final sanity

final sanity

Stories of Lent, Easter, and the Great Fifty Days

Phyllis A. Tickle

THE UPPER ROOM
Nashville, Tennessee

Final Sanity

No part of this book may be used or reproduced in any manner whatsoever
without written permission of the publisher except in brief quotations
embodied in critical articles or reviews. For information address The Upper
Room, 1908 Grand Avenue, P.O. Box 189, Nashville, Tennessee 37202.

All scripture quotations are from the King James Version of the Bible.

"Final Sanity" has appeared in a number of publications, including *The
Tennessee Churchman,* for which it won the Polly Bond Award in 1985.

"Of This April's Showers" has appeared in *The Episcopalian,* as has "So
Much for Walt Disney" in slightly different form.

Selected quotations from the service of Holy Baptism, appearing in "The
Old Priest Grinning," are from *The Book of Common Prayer,* 1979 edition,
published by the Church Hymnal Corporation of New York.

We are grateful to each of these publishers for the use of the materials
reprinted here.

Cover and Book Design: Thelma Whitworth
First Printing: January, 1987 (7)
Library of Congress Catalog Number: 86-50913
ISBN 0-8358-0545-X

Printed in the United States of America

Contents

Prologue 9

A Preface   11

Quinquagesima Sunday   17

1. No Palms in My Purse   19

Mardi Gras   29

2. Living in Stonehenge   31

Ash Wednesday   41

3. Of Swallowtails in Particular   43

Saints' Days: February 24—St. Matthias   51

4. Of Such as I Have   53

March 3—Celebration of John and Charles Wesley   57

5. Too Many Names for Sam   59

Lent   65

6. Final Sanity   67

March 25—The Annunciation   71

7. On Just Such a Morning   73

Holy Week   75

8. The Old Priest Grinning   77

Easter   83

9. Of This April's Showers   85

The Great Fifty Days   91
10. Father and Son   93

April 25—St. Mark   99
11. Through the Veil Torn   101

May 1—St. Philip and St. James   103
12. Patronal Day   105

Rogation Days   109
13. Dance of the Fireflies   111

Ascension Day   115
14. So Much for Walt Disney   117

Postscript   123

Prologue

Holy seasons, like holy days, were not so much invented by the church as they were invented by life itself, I think. By common consent we hold to and preserve that which living has shown us contains the truths of both humankind and God.

I am not a cleric. I have never wanted to study in a seminary or even to have access to one. I am instead a layperson, a writer and editor by trade, a woman. Over my fifty-odd years of living in cities and villages, mill towns and on farms, I have come increasingly to think that every believer must be a kind of psalmist, either literally or privately. That living itself has been given, at least in part, as a way of knowing God intimately. Every event takes on significance in that context, for there is no waste in experience. Every man and woman we meet becomes a metaphor of ourselves; every event, a simile; every thing, a symbol.

As Christians we are taught that our collective understanding and knowledge over the centuries since the coming of God have become, and are contained in, the liturgy and ritual of the church herself, the body of Christ passing itself on to each new member-part in the spiritual codes of symbol and sacrament, ritual and saint. Increasingly I find hope of the shared symbol's becoming once more the common language by which we rear our young, and the mother tongue by which we all will someday cut the lines that separate us from one another.

The essays which follow are true in that they factually report what has happened to me and my family during the days of many holy seasons past. I hope they are true to the mark also in that, in retelling one family's progress toward liturgical truth, they will represent the progress of many, many families toward that same understanding.

We live in a culture still too new to yet have defined itself and under a government so young that my own lifetime has spanned a quarter of its history. In such times and circumstances I have found, in the heritage of the church, a transcendent purpose and connectedness for my own part of creation. For that I have always been grateful. This book is dedicated to the hope that it may be so also for my own children and for those fellow Christians for whom Christianity is both our past and our future.

—From the Prologue to *What the Heart Already Knows*

A Preface

Anybody who has ever written a book or a term paper or even a committee report knows that the respective prefaces or prologues or opening sections were often the last to be written. To use the term "preface" is only one of a myriad of discrepancies that we daily commit between the truth of a thing and the name we give to it. Such misnomers amuse us more than they harm us, and being conventionalized infractions of the truth, they rarely bother our moral sense. Certainly the business of calling my last-written-first-seen pages a "preface" has never bothered mine . . . not, that is, until today.

Today, as I sit to write the opening paragraphs of a book I have finished . . . today, as only these few words stand between me and my mailing off the final manuscript to the Upper Room . . . today, the name "preface" bothers me. These words were not written before the stories which follow them; they are being written now, after the stories have been accumulated. After the stories, written one by one over a span of several years, have told me things I would not have known without them and without the years of living them.

This book and these stories are about Easter. Whatever else they and the events they chronicle may have taught me, they have certainly taught me that Easter is forever. It is a tunnel that has no end, a track running only one way. There is no coming back from Easter to write prefaces, for Easter is never done. It has no getting-off points from which to come back.

So this is not a preface. The paragraphs that follow are no more than a listing of the station calls along the way, a kind of introduction to the scenic spots on a tour for which the church's calendar has for centuries only served as a guide. This is the first whistle-stop for a journey called "Easter."

For convenience the contemporary Christian has come to think of the religious calendar as being divided into only three seasons: Christmas, Easter, and the season after Pentecost (or Ordinary Time). Roughly speaking, Christmas is the liturgical counterpart of nature's winter; Easter is the counterpart of spring; and Ordinary Time takes care of the rest, occurring as it does in the so-called twenty-five or twenty-six green Sundays of summer and fall. While, like most conveniences, this one is a simplification, it is still a highly useful one.

Of the three Christian seasons, Easter is the oldest and the most sacred. It is also the most tightly focused. Technically it is itself composed of Lent, Easter, and the Great Fifty Days, which include Ascensiontide. It begins, for the devout, with what many folk used to call "pre-Lent," but at a popular and widely understood level, it begins with Mardi Gras and Ash Wednesday. It ends with the Feast of Pentecost on the fiftieth and last day of the Great Fifty Days.

In the beginning of things, the Great Fifty Days, which stretch from Easter Morning to Pentecost, were the holy part of the season. With the coming of a number of social and cultural changes during the postmedieval ages and especially with the coming of the church to America, emphasis shifted for several centuries to Lent. Lent had—and has—the singular advantage of giving people something to "do," a very important characteristic for a religion that was passing from its infancy into its adolescence, and even more important for one which was passing into the hands of a merchant class and an urbanized culture. As Christianity and/or America have matured, there has been a gradual tendency to return to the old ways, to the Great Fifty Days, as the center of Eastertide. It is a shift that most of us probably welcome, to the extent that we have even noticed it, and it in no way detracts from the forty days of Lenten preparation. What this change of emphasis does do, however, is make the spring of the church the longest of the holy seasons, taking it from Fat Tuesday for ninety-seven days (or a full calendar quarter) to Pentecost and the beginning of Ordinary Time.

This book, then, is concerned with those ninety-seven days. At least on the face of things it is.

final sanity

Quinquagesima Sunday

In the days of medieval Christianity, the faithful observed a season called "pre-Lent" in which they prepared themselves for the penitential season which was itself designed to prepare them for Easter. Because pre-Lent was almost an elaboration upon an elaboration, it never really commanded much of a place in the hearts and traditions of the church in America. Most of us in this country today, in fact—even those of us from heavily liturgical branches of the faith—take no notice at all of the three weeks that lie between the end of Epiphany and the beginning of Lent . . . except for Quinquagesima Sunday, the last Sunday before Lent.* And Quinquagesima Sunday is remembered, or so my children contend, simply because no one can pronounce it. They may have a point!

Quinquagesima is the Latin word for "fiftieth." Just as *Pentecost,* the Greek word for "fiftieth," became the proper title for the Sunday that comes each year fifty days after Easter and celebrates the coming of Holy

---

*It should be noted that today some church calendars refer to the last Sunday before Lent as Transfiguration Sunday. Transfiguration Sunday appears in August on Roman Catholic and Episcopal church calendars.

Ghost into the Apostles, so Quinquagesima marks the Sunday that lies each year fifty days before Easter and the resurrection of Our Lord. It is, in other words, the twin, the flip side, the other face of Pentecost. Since I truly love to the very core of my being all those nice touches of balance and precision which characterized the ancients, I truly love Quinquagesima for the wrap it makes with Pentecost . . . even if I can't pronounce it without stumbling.

There is, of course, more to Quinquagesima for me than intellectual pleasure over its balancing act. It is, when everything else is said and done, the day when we begin to feel Lent around us. Tuesday will be Mardi Gras and Wednesday will be the imposition of ashes, but Quinquagesima is the day when the palms we held last Palm Sunday are prepared for burning so that their ashes may be used in the Wednesday services. Quinquagesima is also the last Sunday on which we will speak or sing the word *Alleluia* until the resurrection services fifty days down the calendar. The burning of the palms of His triumph and the burying of the resurrection cry become a starkness in my soul that will be matched only on Maundy Thursday, when the altar itself will be stripped and closed for the days of His entombment. It is a somber day of somber events that do indeed foreshadow what the Lenten season must and will be.

$$\boxed{1}$$

No Palms in My Purse

It was a long time ago—ten years this summer, in fact, and half a lifetime of experience. In early May, Nora had gotten married. Our oldest, she was the first of the children to leave us and, according to her father, far too young to have any notion of what she was about. Being quite old enough to know exactly what she was about, she had ceased to argue the point with him and had proceeded, with all due respect and decorum, to get herself married anyway.

By late June and with the wedding bills all paid at last, Sam was still unconsoled and out of sorts because of the hole in his life. I decided it was time to do something—anything—to shake up our routine and interrupt the apparently interminable period of paternal mourning. A vacation seemed in order.

It is a fair measure of my concern that I even mentioned such a thing. Rebecca, our seventh and last acquisition, was not quite two; and the other five still with us were scattered, at various levels of the humanizing process, between her and their now-missing sister. I *hated* family vacations!

At that time in our lives and for obvious reasons, we owned one—actually we had owned and worn out a couple of—those huge, overland Travelalls that International Harvester used to make for folks with our kind of problem. This particular Travelall, however, was still fairly new, and it was certainly still roadworthy. Granny, who lived with us, could no longer sustain the two days of hard driving which lay between us and Florida's Atlantic coast, but I could take her and Rebecca down by plane. Sam could take the other five with him by car, and we would meet in Orlando.

The sea had always—in the days before children—revived both of us. Surely it would do so again. Beginning the trip at Disney World would set just the right tone of excitement and adventure for the children and make them weary enough to enjoy the simpler life of sunning and swimming, which we wanted. At least that was the theory as I proposed it to Sam.

Physicians—my physician husband anyway—don't take many vacations. They may leave town for those seminars and meetings which are necessary to keep them abreast of their field, but neither Sam nor either of his partners has ever been much on being gone for very long at a time. It was a measure of his doldrums, therefore, that he even listened to my proposition. But he did. And like an evil weed, once the idea had been stated out loud, it not only grew, it refused to die.

For one thing, in a house with six children and a grandmother, even words shared in the dark of midnight behind the closed doors of the upper bedroom are heard. They are whispered through the walls and into the hours of the early morning. By noontime they are disseminated, and by the twilight they are fact. It was so with our vacation. At supper of the evening after I had mentioned the idea to Sam, Granny was telling him that two weeks in Florida was exactly what we all needed. He looked accusingly down the table at me, and truly innocent of the charges, I simply shrugged.

He shrugged back. The die was cast, and we were going on vacation.

It took three weeks to arrange the excruciating details of how to be gone from hospital and patients. Who would cover which night was hard enough to establish; the long hours of consultation going over patient charts, worrying about who might possibly get in distress and need what when were impossible. I remembered, listening to it all, why it was that we never took vacations anymore, and it wasn't just having all those children and a grandmother either!

Finally, having managed to arrive at the hottest part of July, we also arrived at the appointed time for leaving. Sam was to pull out on Saturday morning with the Travelall, our gear, and the kids, if he could get them in. Granny, Rebecca, and I would follow on Sunday afternoon. It was, therefore, late Friday afternoon when Sam discovered that, if he got the suitcases, cameras, makeup kits (Mary and Laura were seventeen and fourteen, respectively), potty chairs, floats, books, and coolers into the Travelall, he in fact really couldn't get the kids in.

He made a hasty trip to Sears just at supper and spent fifty desperation dollars to buy what Sears calls, rather inelegantly, a "clam shell." The contrivance is hinged, tracked to sit on top of the luggage racks of big station wagons, and designed to hold everything you ever wanted with room left over for what you could never, ever have need of.

What Sears doesn't tell you, of course, is that once you get the thing in place, get it stuffed, and get it lashed down, you can't open it again until you get where you're going . . . not, that is, unless you want to unlash, unpack, and unload the whole thing all over again. Since this rather obvious (after the fact) point had not been immediately apparent to us, Sam did have to unlash, unpack, and unload just before ten o'clock that Friday night. He showed, I must say, a remarkably negative attitude about the whole thing at the time.

By six o'clock Saturday morning, however, after five hours of muttering sleep—he muttered and slept; I lay beside him and listened—he was ready to pull out with his part of our ménage. He had all the kids except Rebecca, or at least he said he did. I couldn't see any of them through the windows because of all the floats and makeup kits and pillows that he had had to retrieve the night before. But at that point I was willing to take his word for everything, and he was in no mood to be crossed about anything. So he pulled out, leaving me thirty-six hours in which to prepare my soul for the ordeal ahead . . . gird up my loins, so to speak . . . and to repair the damage Daddy and company had left behind.

At not quite two, Rebecca still had a vicious case of that perfectly normal malady—the favorite blanket syndrome. Hers was not a blanket actually. Hers was a wondrously soft patchwork quilt which Mamaw Tickle had fashioned for her out of scraps of old velvet. It was also huge, hot, and filthy—velvet won't wash or even dry-clean very well—but it was necessary. There was no way Rebecca was going to leave that house, much less get on that airplane, without her quilt.

By three o'clock Sunday afternoon, when our plane had missed its connection in Atlanta and there were seven of us to be shuttled in one open cart across the tarmac to the flight Eastern was holding for us, I had developed a strong dislike for Rebecca's equally strong quilt. It had been all over me, the flight attendant, and Granny on the late flight in. Now, in the July heat of central Georgia, it was wrapped solidly across my shoulders . . . the only place I could carry it while holding on to a toddler and a grandmother . . . as our driver careened his way over the perspiring asphalt. By the time we finally deplaned in Orlando, the quilt was thoroughly moist with not only the sweat of my brow but also the end results of a too-long-unchanged diaper. But at least we had no trouble finding more than enough room to ourselves in the back of the motel's airport shuttle. Things were looking up.

By six o'clock a bedraggled Sam was parking the Travelall outside our door, and shortly thereafter our three rooms were threatening to burst. Granny had been assigned the peace of a room with Laura and Mary. Philip had been appointed overseer of the boys' room . . . he mentioned the inequity of these arrangements several times . . . and Daddy and Mama had drawn Rebecca and the quilt.

All three rooms had adjoining doors, so the relegation of goods and people to a particular room lasted only about five minutes. Besides, the Travelall travelers were much too hungry to be interested in unpacking. The last of the suitcases were simply shoved in our door. Just as Sam was locking the door behind us, I thought to open up Rebecca's quilt and drape it over the pile of luggage to air and, I hoped, to dry. Sam locked up and we left.

Dinner, as best I can remember, was one of those really unmemorable affairs one feeds children on the road—lots of hamburgers and french fries and calories—but it was refreshing as were the laughter and silliness that went with it. We really had done the right thing to come after all. I felt a sense of relief that it was all going to work out . . . and a vague hope that the quilt was drying enough so that Rebecca could go right to sleep as soon as we got back to our rooms.

Ice-cream cones in hand, we headed back to the wagon and the motel. Sam was even singing—always a sign of serious well-being—when he unlocked the door for us.

"Ooops! Wrong room!" he said with chagrin, as he backed out and closed it before we could even see in over his shoulder.

He looked at the key, looked at the number on the door in front of us, looked up and down the line of closed doors on either side of us, shook his head, and looked back at the door.

"I don't understand. It's the right number."

He inserted the key and opened the door again. This time we all crowded in behind him. The room looked just fine to me. Just like the one we had left . . . but not just like we had left it! Except for the usual furniture, there was nothing in it! No luggage, no coolers, and no quilt!

There had to be a mistake. The motel must have moved us while we were at supper. Sam went to the phone to call the desk. Philip meanwhile went into the boys' room and announced that everything there was just as they had left it. There couldn't be a mistake. Laura, in turn, discovered all of the girls' gear still in place in their room.

The desk was as surprised as we were . . . or at least the young lady behind it was. It took no more than two minutes, however, for the manager to make it out of the office and around to our room. He was *not* surprised.

They had had a rash of break-ins the past two weeks . . . apparently a disgruntled former employee trying to ruin the motel . . . taking everything, even the silliest things ("Wet baby quilts, for instance?" I asked), more to anger patrons than to steal . . . in fact, they had found some of the suitcases in the dumpsters around town. . . . The upshot was that he was very sorry, a condition no one was denying him at that point. The motel would of course like to have us as its guests without charge for our stay and would make such restitution as it could of our goods, a point which Rebecca began immediately to deny him, for it was at that point that it dawned on her what had happened.

She howled, and the beleaguered manager, having said all he could say, backed his way toward the door, assuring Sam that it would be easier for everyone . . . he nodded in my direction . . . if the two of them were to step down to his office to call the police and complete the necessary papers.

Mary astutely took Granny to bed, and Philip discovered an absolutely compelling cops-and-robbers show on the boys' TV. Both had the charity to leave their doors open, should I get into real trouble, but neither offered much encouragement beyond a knowing shake of the head.

The howling diminished to wails, and the wails were interrupted with "I want my quilt!" but there was to be no ready diminishment of her grief. I could hear the sirens downstairs in the parking lot, and through the crack in the drapes I could see the blue lights flashing. Three cars. Poor Sam. He could be at this all night. Rebecca wailed. Poor me. I would be at this all night!

During the next half hour, I rocked, Rebecca cried, and Sam, Jr.—just-turned-five and always the tender one in the family—wandered wistfully back and forth between our two rooms. He stood finally in the doorway between, watching Rebecca with a distress on his face as real as that which she seemed to be feeling. From time to time, he would come to us, stroke her face with his pudgy, little-boy hand, and then leave. He never told her to hush or that it would be all right. Stranded in that space between his own babyhood and the boy toward whom he was growing, he still remembered his own quilt. Of all of us, he most knew it would indeed not be all right.

Sam came back, tired, frustrated, but in good humor. It had happened, and it was over. His concern now was all for Rebecca and/or getting everyone bedded down for a big day tomorrow despite her distress. I rocked and he marshaled, so that in a relatively brief time all was quiet, save for the sniffling baby in my arms. He lay down, and in the quiet, Rebecca began to croon, "I want my quilt, Mommy, I want my quilt. I want my quilt, Mommy, I want my quilt," over and over.

"Hush, now, Baby. We'll get you a new quilt. Mamaw will make you a new quilt."

"I want my quilt, Mommy, I want my quilt," as if she had not even heard me.

"Mamaw will make you another quilt, Baby. Go to sleep now, and tomorrow we will call Mamaw to make you a new quilt."

"I want my quilt, Mommy, I want my quilt."

"Mamaw will make you a quilt. . . . "

"Don't tell her that." Sam, Jr., was standing in the dark just inside our room. "It won't do any good. A new one won't have her dreams in it." Then he was gone, a little piece of boy in white underwear and no pajamas.

I rocked on after that until the crooning stopped and Rebecca drifted, weary beyond even her own grief.

The next morning all was sunshine and Mickey Mouse. We called Mamaw, and either Rebecca understood what we were doing or she was simply resigned. She whimpered at naptime and again at bedtime, but the wailing was over and the vacation, so eventful in its beginnings, was almost ordinary in its ending. Fully rested and revived, we returned, two weeks later, to home and a waiting parcel that held a smaller, more hastily made, but nonetheless velvet, quilt from Mamaw.

Sam, Jr., was right, of course. Rebecca watched as

Mary unwrapped the box and lifted out the new quilt. She took it and smiled as she buried her face in its softness. She even sighed as she slid off my lap and snuggled down on the floor with it. But it was almost a year before she loved it—before she had put enough dreams into it to need it.

Sam, Jr., is fourteen now . . . soon fifteen . . . and taller than I, but still the tender one. Almost to manhood and strong as his father, he still stands sometimes, more than any of the others, in that space between remembering and growing.

Each Palm Sunday, before we begin the final hymns of the Triumphal Entry, our priest elevates the palm fronds that have been used to decorate the altar, blesses them, and hands them to the ushers. As we pass, singing toward the front of the nave, each of us takes and carries out onto the parish lawn a single frond. When the hymns are done, the procession finished, and the benediction shouted above the chatter of the birds and the excitement of the children, we go our separate ways, each carrying a frond into the coming year. I will carry mine . . . as, until recently, I always carried the children's, too . . . in a pouch in my purse. There, from time to time, I will sometimes deliberately seek it; and there, by its mere presence, it will from day to day remind me of why I am here . . .

. . . until next spring when, as they do each year on Quinquagesima Sunday, the women of the Altar Guild will stand near the church door, their hands out to take back our palms from the various pouches and pockets and Bibles where we have harbored them for almost a year. The minute I see them standing there, I am filled with the desire to turn back or to slip by, to this year not let go of my frond. Tuesday, in this same building, it and all the others like it will be burned, their ashes saved against the coming of Ash Wednesday services. From now until then, I will have no palms at all, and from now until Palm Sunday, seven weeks away, I will have no frond. But because I am not yet old enough to be candid, I turn mine in as dutifully as I always have and go away saddened by a loss I will not feel again until next year, and of which I will not be entirely relieved even on Palm Sunday.

Last year was the first time Sam, Jr., had wanted to keep his palm himself. I agreed, as I have with all the other children, that it was time. When we came, then, to Quinquagesima this spring and the Altar Guild, I watched as he pulled out his frond from the shirt pocket under his sweater. He hesitated before he handed it over. When he realized I had seen him, he ducked his head. "It's a lot like Rebecca's quilt," he said by way of apology. "Full of dreams."

Well, I thought to myself, *I didn't know he had remembered after all these years, but I certainly should have known that he understood.*

Mardi Gras

Mardi Gras has always seemed to me to be one of the more stellar examples of the church's wisdom. While most of us in this country know the day by its French name because of the New Orleans experience, its English translation or name is equally engaging, at least to me—Fat Tuesday—and that certainly reflects most accurately its immediate, physical result.

In the old days before adequate refrigeration, the Christian wife had to arrange, on this last day before Lent, the total consumption of all the delicious and sinful foods in her larder. (We are talking here pure country butter, sage-laced sausage, and moist lumps of brown maple sugar, among other delectables). They had to be either eaten or destroyed before Ash Wednesday came. The result was one of the world's most incredible feasts; and any nutritionist will tell you what all those calories in one day will lead to . . . drinking, dancing, and riotous living.

Our times are a bit more restrained, despite how the television coverage of New Orleans may make things appear to the contrary. We no longer have to consume everything in sight . . . not only because we have refrigeration, but also because we no longer keep Lent.

It's a handy adaptation. The old ways, nonetheless, have hung on, and with considerable ecclesiastical encouragement.

In many American churches Fat Tuesday is still the night when the whole parish gathers in the church kitchen for pancakes and sausage (same menu, you see) and then enjoys games and singing (secular) after supper. I never saw a parish Fat Tuesday that actually served enough pancakes or maple syrup to tip me or anyone else over into caloric insanity; but most Americans, I suspect, who first observe the day in their church kitchens do their real feasting and dancing after, and away from, the parish festival. However all of that may be, the carnival has stayed, and it is the carnival that most attests the church's wisdom.

All of us who arrive at spiritual maturity arrive by moving through a progression of faiths and comprehensions. In much the same way, all of us who now walk had first to move through a fairly unoriginal progression of motor skills before we arrived at our walking. In effect, what the process leaves most of us with is a veritable pantheon of early gods and codes, discarded in our maturity, but essential to our growth—gods and understandings that led us to Easter in the first place.

Mardi Gras with its carnival and its homage to the pagan is the church's recognition of that fact. It is also a recognition of the spiritual necessity for primordial darkness, and of the uses of the other side of light. It is our chance to remember, one time a year and with sanction, the long way of our coming and the strange way of our arriving. In its own way and used with faith, it is one of the most instructive holidays of the church's year.

2

Living in Stonehenge

Our only near neighbor put in a wood-burning furnace last year, an incredible contrivance whose like I had never seen before and whose functions have proved to be a source of constant family conversation. The furnace itself—a freestanding box of sizable proportions—is situated . . . or, as the children say, got plopped . . . on our side of our neighbor's house where we could, with delicacy and complete discretion, watch every part of its installation. We have, of course, continued to watch every part of its use as well, also with complete discretion.

The best we can tell from here, the air thus heated runs through an underground pipe over to the central air conditioning system where, by some method never apparent to one husband and two sons and three sons-in-law, the central air motor and ducts convey it into the house for circulation. Not being mechanical or even bent in that direction, I care not at all about how the blessed thing works, but I am fascinated by such juxtaposing of central air conditioning and primitive heating. I am also downright entertained by all the ways in which primitive heating can command the energies of its owners.

The first thing we noticed was that an electric light had been strung out the kitchen window and attached to the body of the furnace. It took two nights and one late call to the hospital for Sam to discover that the lamp was there to illuminate the furnace's 2:00 A.M. feeding. I can remember that light helps in such matters.

The next thing was that the W.'s tractor, which had heretofore always been carefully parked in the lean-to of the barn, now stayed out all the time in the side yard beside the furnace box. Apparently pulling the flatbeds of wood up to the box and of ashcans away from it became a frequent-enough event to discourage even Mr. W. from parking and unparking the tractor a half-a-farm away. *Interesting,* I think, every time I watch yet another load of wood being brought in and left just beside the furnace door.

By early December of last year, our first truly cold month with the furnace, our neighbor had begun to show a serious interest in pruning his trees. The first ones to go were down in the back pasture, and they probably really did need to go. But when Mr. W. started topping an oak in his front acreage, the children whooped and Saturday lunch was delayed for an hour while they watched the process.

Country children or not, our youngsters are each and every one dedicated to creature comforts, and electric heat is number one on their list of creature comforts. Sam, in contrast, has long been notorious for his attempts to remain ecologically in balance, by which he means independent of outside sources for our necessities. Apparently the near presence of yet another method of being ecologically balanced seriously threatened the children's sense of well-being, especially the boys', who could foresee hours of chopping and loading should the monster prove workable. This final evidence of kinks in the scheme of things delighted them beyond anything last year save Christmas itself.

Since the oak topping, they have been free to both observe and comment with impunity. There was, in particular, considerable wagering last winter on whether Mr. W. would leave the thing in place once spring finally came, or whether he would retire Old Beelzebub (their name) to the nether reaches from whence he had come. So in the weeks of last March and April, as the days grew warmer and the evenings less and less chilly, I found myself more anxious about, than interested in, Beelzebub's fate. It was an enormous relief to me, then, when Mr. W. had the generosity not only to leave Beelzebub in place all summer, but also to fire him up with the first chilly evenings of this past fall.

Over the dull months of two winters and the long weeks of one Lent I have grown accustomed to Beelzebub, maybe even fond of him. His smokestack, which sits no more than three feet high, constantly emits a lazy spiral of smoke which is not unattractive in and of itself. In addition, the odor of the burning wood is so pervasive as to scent pleasantly every part of our house. It's rather like living in a Christmas-card world all winter actually, and I would miss it now, were it not here.

But mainly I would miss Beelzebub's information. Unlike the children, I am here all day, my office window looking right out into Old Beelzebub's face; and I have come to count on him as thermometer, wind sock, and snow gauge. In our almost-two winters together, he has not been wrong yet. When the stack bellows with smoke, it's too cold to go out without a shawl or wrap. When the smoke blows north toward Mr. W.'s orchard, it's going to be sunny. When it blows south toward the highway, it's going to be much colder before suppertime. And, alas, when it blows east toward us, anything can happen; and whatever it is, neither we nor the stock are going to like it much. The happiest choice for me, since I'm still a child at heart, is for the smoke to crawl out of Beelzebub's stack, hesitate, and then slink down the box, hurrying away just above ground level. That one means snow, and I feel as giddy as the Cumaean sibyl telling her vapors when, at twilight, the wet flakes begin to fall.

Obviously all this same information . . . and with almost the same degree of accuracy . . . could be got by listening to our NOAA station or by tuning in to the evening television news, but I'm like Sam. I like to stay ecologically balanced. Besides, Beelzebub is a much more romantic prognosticator than NOAA, in addition to being easier to consult.

So, subtly and noontime-by-noontime, Beelzebub has stolen his way into my affections and my habits, and I am honestly glad of his survival and ongoing good health. He has become part of our scheme of things, rather like Stonehenge.

"Stonehenge" is Sam's name for our bedroom. The room itself was originally two rooms, both of an adequate but apparently inelegant size. At some point some previous owner took out the separating wall and created a space more comparable to a double garage than to a bedroom. The resulting space has one window facing east by northeast; two facing east by southeast; and two facing almost directly south.

The first year of our living here, I luxuriated in the spaciousness of our quarters—this was what Mama had always meant by "master bedroom"—and the glories of the southern windows. Every plant or flower or vine that I set in front of them would instantly respond by thriving to incredible lushness and vigor. Nothing in the plant world that could not be revived or nursed back to health by a week in the bedroom windows! But while I was busy puttering with plant life, Sam was busy with other matters.

It was during our second winter here that he began curiously to make marks on the western, and only solid, wall of the bedroom. Lying in bed in the mornings in the soft time between waking and rousing, he would roll over toward the wall and, with his finger, make a faint smudge on the white paint. Then he would get up and set about his chores as if nothing unusual had happened. It was the third week of June that second year and the morning after the summer solstice when he first said, "Stonehenge!" Actually, what he did was, he woke up, rolled to the wall as usual, and then exclaimed, "Ah, hah! Just as I thought. Stonehenge!"

Over the winter months his smudges had progressed northward along our western wall to its farthest point at the head of our bed and around the corner onto the northern wall against which the bed sits. But this morning the next-to-the-last smudge, which Sam had made two days before, was glowing in the slit of early morning light which comes in around the shades. Even befogged by sleep, I could still share his excitement . . . by removing the wall, someone before us, either knowingly or accidentally, had created a highly accurate astrological device. And Stonehenge our room has been ever since.

While no one would ever find our bedroom wall more useful than the almanac, or even more accessible in this case, and while even Sam confesses that this is carrying ecologically balanced living a bit far, there is something very comforting about knowing that one can calculate without a calendar. There is also something very intellectually reassuring about knowing, from personal and diurnal experience, the awe of the ancient mysteries. What the books relate about the

Celtic priests on the plains of Salisbury is as nothing emotionally to the effect of watching Sam's sliver of light move each winter north up the room and then, turning, come back south to midwall for Christmas.

More than that, of course, there is the immediacy of Old Beelzebub's smoke and of Sam's smudges which grants us the grace of unstudied knowing and leaves us childlike in the directness of our connection with seasons and solstice. Stonehenge and Beelzebub have become portals for us, just as their precursors were for the ancients, by which the natural mysteries slip into us, joining us with the intimacy of bedroom and workplace.

The children treasure Stonehenge, in particular, it having proved to be an easier union for them, especially in early adolescence, than the Mass where the crucified God enters the divine Self into their food. Their seriousness of purpose, in fact, and the deliberateness of their ponderings are not unlike those that I learned as a child playing alone in my bedroom closet.

Huge in its dimensions and cavernous with its ten-foot ceiling, the closet of my girlhood, while it still existed, was once full of mothballs and almost-dispatched toys, my mother's perfume, cedar boxes, and my father's collection of newspapers . . . one for every day of the Second World War from Pearl Harbor to Hiroshima. Everything in that closet was planned and preserved for its utility. Even the shelves were so spaced as to make an uneasy ladder up to the forbidden trap door that opened onto insulation and crawl space.

It was always, from the beginning, the closet in which I arranged and stored myself. I was the one who threw out its excess, wrought order upon its collections, sorted its debris for the raw materials of my soul's education. Whatever parent or cousin or time dumped, I sorted by feel in the dark or by stealth with a flashlight, spiriting out the useless to the alley trash bins and climbing to the top shelf repository with the remains. There neither my short-of-stature mother nor my taller-but-less-inquisitive father ever could or would go.

The closet was pantheon for my childhood's gods. It was as full of personalities as was my father's copy of the *Inferno*, illustrated by Doré and secreted years before on the upper shelf, much to my father's recurring puzzlement. The upper shelf's walls sang with awesome pictures of Shiva, Astarte, Hecate, etc., . . . all torn from the pages of my grandmother's discarded *Chamber's Illustrated Encyclopedia*. A china Ferdinand the Bull, which my uncle had brought me from New York, shared the closet's fantasia with crayoned tracings of satyrs much less benign than those Walt Disney would have wanted me to believe in. And the arms of the goddess Kali (brass and beautiful from India but repugnant to my mother, who had thrown her away) waxed over the whole of the shelf in constant incantation.

Somewhere just near the attic crawl-through was God the Father, his beard frequently no more than a cobweb; but still he was there—or passage to him was. Even as a child I knew that there was no God the Mother and was glad. I did not want one. Gentleness, nurture, support, stroking were sexless in my understanding, belonging to neither gender exclusively and to both identically. It was Kali with her many-handed sexuality whom I wanted as the Queen of Forever. It was Kali who helped me hone the diffuse appetites of youth into focus.

Kali was the only one of the closet's treasures to escape its destruction. She alone still sits on my bedroom dressing table. All the rest have long since gone as victims to my own maturing or the house's new owners. I threw Shiva and Astarte away before I was fully ten years old. In high school I had to study Dante and, for convenience, moved him back down to the more accessible bookshelf. Doré's ghouls and phantasmagoria by that time were more eternally etched into my faith than they ever could have been into the pages of any book. Ferdinand I had broken one adolescent day by hurling him against a brick wall. In a rush of need to know what it was to kill someone I truly loved, I had hurled him away from me. Even today I can still feel the slick heat of him as he slid from my hand to his multifaceted destruction. Like so many toys for so many children, he served me better in death than in life, and I never mourned him. Bit by bit and doll by doll, the other treasures were carried out and dispersed to other children, to nieces, nephews, neighbors, some even to my own children.

During Vietnam and not long before his death, my father burned his World War II collection. It was after his funeral and before we sold the house that I finally moved Kali out of the closet and to her place on the dresser in the Stonehenge.

Tonight we will symbolically lay away the foods of rich energy and begin tomorrow the lean diet of bland restriction that we may the better, in these coming weeks of many communions, taste and know our God. When I was an undergraduate, I was taught in some psychology class or other that the most definitive difference between a philosophy and a religion is that the latter requires the eating of the atonement sacrifice, while the former is revulsed by such notions. It was a hard lesson for me then, for I was myself still an adolescent. Now I am older, come to middle life, grown simpler.

As I wait now for our youngest and last three to finish dressing for parish supper, I remember my own ambivalence at their ages—excitement for the pancakes and fun, fear for the coming time of frequent eucharists. For me, I think, it was easier because of Kali; and for them, because of Stonehenge and even because of Old Beelzebub, too.

Grateful, I look out and see his smoke running just above the ground toward us.

"Get your boots too, Kids! It'll be snowing before we get back home!"

The Holy Season has begun.

Ash Wednesday

Ash Wednesday is probably the one day in the Christian year that has ever bothered our children. The thing itself is fairly simple. The palms they loved carrying in procession last year on Palm Sunday have been burned to make ashes, and those ashes have been blessed, before Ash Wednesday begins. Whether we gather at the 7:30 service in the morning or at the midday service or, as occasionally happens, we have to attend the evening service in order to all be together, the end result is always the same.

We move through the service as if this were just any other day of the year until, following the communion, the congregation returns to the altar rail for the imposition of the ashes. Putting his thumb in the small dish he carries, the priest moves in front of us, making the sign of the cross on each forehead.

It is the only time of the year that we are ever marked, that on our bodies we carry the sign of the faith. Both ancient and primitive, the marks will stay with us throughout the day. It is the manner of their acceptance of the sign, then, that tells Sam and me where a child is in understanding what it means to say, "I am Christian."

3

Of Swallowtails in Particular

The last chores of the day are always bathroom chores for me—collecting all the wet towels and shucked underwear for one last trip down to the laundry room; rubbing on the cleansing cream that freezes me even in the summertime and then rubbing it and my makeup off again; rinsing one last ring out of the tub before I crawl in myself for the warm soak that eases my body into sleeping and my day into summary.

I suspect, truth told, that the bathrooms in a lot of houses function in the same way that this one does; that their principal function has never really been the declared business of cleanliness and hygiene.

In the early days when there were many of us at home, the bathroom was the prize as well as the sanctuary. If you got up early enough or stayed awake late enough, you had a chance of getting a bath instead of a shower. With any luck you could even wash your hair at the same time instead of having to hang your head over the mop sink in the laundry room later.

Like all parents of many children . . . or of just one if that one is a four-year-old . . . Sam and I have spent our fair share of time hiding in the bathrooms of our various houses past as I am now hiding in this one. Some of my most credible thoughts, certainly, have come in those midnight tubs when everyone and everything, including the last of the hot water, have gone away for the day.

But our crowding and our need for sanctuary have changed over the last few years. We are down now to only five of us at home, with three bathrooms . . . this one for Sam and me, one downstairs for the two boys, and—luxury of luxury—one for Rebecca all to herself. It is her bathroom that most persuades me that overcrowding and overactivity were never the real reason for our bathroom retreats.

Becca does everything in her bathroom . . . half her daytime life is conducted from there. She paints by the hour—all over the farm—but the lab in which the paints are both mixed and stored is her bathroom. A perfumer at heart, she has, for as long as she has been able to reach the bathroom sink from her little wooden stepstool, mixed the petals of every flower she and her father grow. She soaks them for days in concoctions that only the two of them know the bases of, because Daddy's the one who, up in her bathroom, showed her what glycerin would do, and alcohol, and even beeswax and lanolin. When she was ten, her experiments into the essences that can be thus extracted and/or suspended would have done honor to a much older practitioner; and her ongoing pleasure in her experimentation has been so pervasive over the years that I have tolerated the mess in fascination, cleaning up around, rather than through, it.

Originally the perfuming began as a result of flower collecting. By the time she was six she simply could not let the flowers die in the fall. More and more of them were picked and brought into the bathroom to be cajoled into extended life by every means she could contrive. At first she simply made crude pomanders that always molded. By the time she was eight she had managed to assemble three flower presses in the bathroom: one she annoyed an older sister into buying for her; one she made for herself by the simple process of nagging John until he cut the boards and drilled the holes for her; and one she got by default when Laura Lee married and moved away. In just a few months after that last acquisition, she progressed from pressing to drying and from drying to preserving. Mason jars of noxious deterrents to vegetative death lined the tile floor in front of her shower stall so that, while taking a shower was still possible, climbing back out was a definite hazard.

All of which would have been domestically tolerable if the function of her bathroom hadn't moved from flowers to creatures. At first it was daddy longlegs, which was fine and even normal. After seven children I regard granddaddy-longlegs all over one's bathrooms as almost ordinary, in fact. Then it was praying mantises, which was sort of on the money too. Then we got to the snails . . . twenty-two of them at one point . . . also in the shower stall. There seemed to be no real reason for having collected them . . . they were just there, rather like Mount Everest to a climber. But watching them must have conveyed something, however subliminal, because they were replaced in just one summer by caterpillars.

There was none of the true biologist's absorption in cataloging and categorizing. Not with this child. Any caterpillar would do, just as long as it crawled and was stupid enough to be outside when Becca was. At ten . . . which she was summer before last when this particular wave of perversion overtook us . . . she wasn't even enough of a student to consider the probability of stingers, and she paid a time or two. Whatever else she may have learned or not learned from the summer of the

caterpillars, she surely learned which ones not to ha-
rass, at least not with her bare fingers.

The captive caterpillars were all housed with a kind
of naive abandon about natural sympathies and ani-
mosities. As a result, I have to report that some of them
were eaten by others of them; but the mason jars that
had previously held the noxious chemicals were once
more lined up in front of the shower stall, filled this time
with caterpillars and eventually with cocoons.

There is a kind of phlox that looks a bit like butterfly
bush but seems to be more nourishing. Rebecca and
her father grow the stuff in every available inch of flower
bed around the patio and along the back of the house. It
has allowed them to entice literally dozens of hum-
mingbirds near the windows of the kitchen where we
eat. The bumblebees are intoxicated into apparent ecstasy by the pollen. But it is the butterflies which have
proved to be incredibly varied and numerous in their
feedings. Sometimes in the late afternoons of July and
August all of the patio beds appear to be on the wing,
so great is the activity.

It was, naturally then, the phlox that Rebecca decided to feed to her caterpillar horde. Day after day that
summer handsful of the purply stalks went through the
kitchen and up the hall to the bathroom. Day after day I
followed behind her, picking up a trail of fallen purple
petals. From the back door through the kitchen and up
the stairs to Becca's room I went twice a day, complaining every step of the way about kids and their messes
. . . all the while wondering to myself whether I was
indeed soft enough and traditional enough to be putting up with all of this simply because she was the baby
and I was going to miss having them around me. I
finally decided that I was and I would. It was a depress-
ing discovery after all these years of saying, "I can
hardly wait, Lord! I can hardly wait!"

The caterpillars, meanwhile, were fed unreal amounts of phlox, and those that weren't themselves eaten all thrived. In fact, just going into Becca's bathroom got to be a scary thing. The boys, who in the past had really rather resented her status of single owner and had pestered her frequently for the right to use her shower on hot evenings, gradually lost all interest in even trying to get in. The rewards were totally canceled by the experience of having all those jars of crawling eyes see you buck-naked . . . or that's what John told me one night when I asked him why he didn't use Becca's shower to clean up anymore.

So the summer waned into fall, and the fall showed every sign of waning into winter, and the cocoons came. Now the jars were full of depending paper sackettes. This thing was getting interesting even to me. To everyone's amazement, including my own, I cleared off the back of the water closet and made a kind of shelf for the jars so I could see them better. I think I also had some notion that the light and the cycle of day and night might be essential to the proper development of whatever it is that happens to a pupa, but I would never have admitted to Rebecca that that was my motivation. I simply claimed a parental weariness with all those jars that made mopping the floor impossible (at this point, the tile floor really had achieved an impressive layer of purple rot in front of the shower door).

The winter came and left. Then, in mid-April of last year, we discovered that while Rebecca might not be much as a cataloger of collections, she had nonetheless stored in her head a complete inventory of which caterpillars had made which cocoons.

"What do you mean, that one is going to be a swallowtail?" I asked her one afternoon in amazement when she moved one of the jars downstairs into the kitchen so we all could watch it.

"Well, I think that's what it will make." She was answering me with less sureness than she usually has when challenged. "It had those two sets of dark hairs like a swallowtail should have when it's a worm."

I knew I probably wanted to let that one alone, but she picked up a pencil anyway and drew me a picture of the caterpillar she had captured, saying, "See, this right here should become this right here," and the bug sketched into a butterfly under her pencil.

"I'm not sure it works that way," I objected.

"Neither am I. That's why it's down here."

By Tuesday of Holy Week—the afternoon that the thing finally hatched—I was prepared to be all emotional and motherly about the event. She came in from school to the jar and the emerging butterfly that I had been watching for the better part of a half hour. She sat down and began to observe the last stages of the process without a word being said. *Well*, I thought, *let her alone. She'll talk when she wants to* (never a problem with Rebecca), and I went upstairs. In a little while I heard the back door slam and then slam again. The water went on in the kitchen, and I couldn't stand it any longer. I went down, and there she was, washing out the jar.

"What happened?" I asked.

"I let it go. It was a swallowtail just like I thought . . . had to be because of the markings. Stuff like that doesn't change just because you can't see it."

She could not have been more indifferent. I have always questioned all the butterflies on church bulletins and Easter cards, and I have doubted, even more, all the butterflies that get hung about in some kind of anxious homage to a vague hereafter; yet I simply could not ignore this child's cavalier treatment of the biggest cliché in popular religion, especially not right in the middle of Holy Week itself.

"But, Becca, the caterpillar died to make that butterfly! Don't you think you should at least care a little bit about that?"

She shook her head. "No, ma'am, I think that whatever died, died so the markings would live."

She started drying the still cloudy jar with my clean tea towel. "The markings were what mattered. They made it a swallowtail," and she walked off carrying the jar with her back up to her bathroom. I rehung the rumpled towel and forgot about Becca and the swallowtail . . . until tonight.

This day began early for us as it does every year on Ash Wednesday . . . up before the clock for 7:30 services and the imposition of ashes, the ashes that are still drawn black and heavy across my forehead. But tonight as I reach for the cleansing cream, my prayer is simpler than in years passed.

"Father, let her be right. Let me have been about markings all along."

Saints' Days

February 24—St. Matthias

Probably no part of traditional or historic Christianity has caused more dissension than has the keeping or observing of saints' days. Most of us who are Protestant by heritage were reared to regard all the saints as suspect at the very least and papist at the very worst. On the other hand, if one can believe my Roman friends, our lack of reverence for the great leaders of the faith which has characterized decades of American Protestantism seems to them and to their parents to be arrogant at the very least and blatantly heretical at the very worst. It is an arresting conflict of opinion which has also, over the years, become a kind of symbol, the outward and visible sign, of very substantial differences; and the one on which the two divisions of the faith early fixed as a kind of wrestling ground.

Equally arresting has been the way our two divisions have attempted lately to soften the dissension about saints' days as a means of softening the impact of our other differences. Notably, the Roman division of the church has decreased the sheer number of saints, thereby lending the whole thing credibility, while the Protestant division has increased its attention to the heroes of the faith, even daring to call some of them by the name of saint. Certainly we all seem now to agree that the Apostles and the Evangelists are acceptable material for emulation and study. Most of us even agree that they constitute legitimate sources of names for our churches or our ladies' groups or our service guilds. It's an interesting step forward, to say the least.

Lent and Easter have four saints' days which honor five men: St. Matthias, the Apostle (February 24); St. Joseph (March 19); St. Mark, the Evangelist (April 25); and the Apostles, St. Philip and St. James (May 1).

While none of these, unless it is a patronal day, is kept in this country by any significant system of observation beyond the appropriate readings for the day, it does seem that all of us—Protestant, Roman, and Eastern Orthodox alike—have some vested interest in calling to mind those who, unlike most of us, did manage to see a different world and live this life within it. It is an appreciation—if one may call it that—which, despite being Protestant, I still deliberately call to mind at least once a year on St. Philip's Day, that being my own patronal day, and randomly on other saints' days. The latter observations usually occur, I must confess, when some purely gratuitous, external event ties itself to the day.

4

Of Such as I Have

The sky was petulant when we got up this morning, churning itself above us, as heavy and pulpy as *papier-mâché*. Even while I did my morning chores among them, the animals were as silent as the day, their conversations limited to Alouette's mew for her kittens and an occasional cry from the drake. In the far pasture I could see the cows herded against the close, half of them still standing lest they be caught unprepared by what they were restless to hear.

The hours of our early morning have all been used up now in our waiting. Knowing better, and more from habit than wisdom, I sit down here at my desk, pretending to myself that I shall work a while. Instead I stare out the window. I watch. Like the cows, I fear what we are waiting for.

A draft from off the river, ten miles to the west of us, moved across the yard a few minutes ago. It tossed Sam's forsythia bushes and lifted his holly branches momentarily. In delight and false relief, my favorite woodpecker sailed across from one pine tree to another. But the wind died, and he has once more assumed his silent posture atop the new tree. He too is waiting, and I ponder, disinterestedly, whether or not the grubs he usually hears in the pine bark are also silent today, whether or not they too are waiting.

Water begins to drip off the corner of the gutter and down into the flower bed—condensation too cool to make rain, too sparse to find the downspout. Finally, as if shamed by his own fear, Dublin rises stiffly to his gatepost, hesitates, and at last sounds the day. The hens follow his noise into the fowl lot, pecking and scratching without enthusiasm as they come. Seeing them below him, Dublin escapes from his perch into the freedom of the farmyard.

Two butterflies begin mating above the kitchen flower bed. One by one, they are joined from nowhere by five more. The guineas come wandering up the path from the orchard, beeping and barking crossly as they come; and the ducks rise, in a hurry suddenly to get to the feed trays beyond the patio before the guineas do. As always, the ducks lose, giving up the race with angry quacking and agitation. Like a great patriarch, Dublin tries to scold them all into silence, but to no avail. Neither guineas nor ducks will be instructed by a chicken, not even by one who is a friend.

Abruptly from across the fields I hear a motor—a tractor, probably—kick off and begin to drone. I sigh with relief. So many times before I have seen it all happen, have witnessed this subtle end to waiting, that I know by heart how the rest of the day will undo itself now. Shortly the cows will change their position from the close to the open hillocks above the pond; the woodpecker will hear his grubs at last and go after them; the phone will ring. I start back toward my work.

The yellowish gray outside my study windows begins to lift itself away. Already the trees beyond the fence are clearer. Soon they will be florescent in their greening bark. As I talk to some man on the phone about why we don't want solar heating installed, or whatever it is he is trying to sell, I can see the trees begin to move comfortably again, their tops bending, ever so slightly but ever so consistently, back and forth in the breeze that must have come up just as I began talking. The call cared for, I begin to move through the house, closing windows, grateful that, in the final analysis, today was still too cool to make the tornado we almost had.

Somewhere upriver the weather that has passed over us will be shaped by the heat of the late winter earth, will focus, and will destroy with a fury increased by our having denied it. Dublin crows again, I assume for the sheer raucousness of the crow. Even he must know by now that no one is paying him any mind at all. The sun comes through the trees, its light winking at me from the water troughs. Our tornado has indeed moved beyond us.

In my sun-bright office with a breeze lightly singing in the eaves above me, I sit back down and play from experience the footage the television will run tonight. The leveled trailer park, its pieces strewn across perfectly flat land. The aerial shots, including the especially long one of a shopping mall deroofed. At least one tree-blocked section of interstate and, of course, one broken and discolored doll caught on the jagged edge of wreckage.

That's where our storm has gone . . . where it has been carried by our sophistication. I have lost it already in the predictability of the package by which it will be returned to me. In the inevitability of its targets. In the clichés and maudlin metaphors of its about-to-be television life. Somewhere upriver, in western Kentucky or southern Illinois or central Ohio, some part of us is going to have a bitter afternoon, have individual reason to remember this St. Matthias' Day for the rest of time, and I can only think of, not feel with, them.

All the natural and cultivated barriers which information can throw up against feeling rise now to insulate me. So much space and so many differences of circumstance protect me. Even memory refuses to relieve my impotence, and I, listening now to my woodpecker hammering away for his grubs, can no longer feel how viciously his silence oppressed me not fully thirty minutes ago. I can remember only that it did.

Pain in all its forms—loss, grief, depression, agony—is much too intense in its presence and much too unimaginable in its absence for any of us to have many pretensions about it, I suppose, except to know that it is the one barrier which really does separate us. That it is the impassable moat which surrounds each person's castle and denies entrance to each person's center. Yet, that denial and that separation are themselves a kind of pain for those of us who wait outside the moat, cut off by it.

So as I wait here . . . wait to hear . . . wait to know . . . wait for the evening news I deplore, I think I must know how the Apostles felt. I have nothing to give, but of such as I have, give I unto you . . . words. I give you words this St. Matthias' Day to say I care.

March 3—
Celebration of John and Charles Wesley

One way to ameliorate the problem of saints' days as a bone of contention is to add some nonsaints' days to the liturgical calendar. This has certain inherent problems, of course. In the first place, nonsaints seem odd things for good Christian folk to honor; and as any priest will quickly tell you, commemoration days for nonsaints hardly hold a candle (pun intended) to feast days for saints. Nonetheless, some of us keep trying, most notably the Episcopal church, which is my own particular brand of the faith.

Standing as it does somewhere between pure Protestantism and pure Catholicism, the Episcopal body of Christ has the greatest freedom to hold both commemorations and feasts. It also has the greatest hope of making both experiences meaningful for its congregants. It has, therefore, long been the custom of the church to set aside certain days on its calendar to reverence the godly acts of great people of the faith who, because of their private persuasions, will never be denominated as saints per se. None of the notable people who fall in this category are more consistently remembered or have their day more consistently observed than John and Charles Wesley.

If one can believe history, both John and Charles, to the day of their deaths, regarded themselves as good Anglicans and good priests. The fact that later times have stuck the term "Methodist" permanently to the form of Christianity which grew up from their work and their faith never affected their own perception of themselves.

John Wesley died on March 3, 1791, and March 3 is marked on the Anglican calendar as the Commemoration of John and Charles Wesley, not because of their Anglicanism, but because of their Methodism. On that day, the devout remember and are grateful for two men of God who, seeing a new world, new times, and new ways growing up around them, found the grace to adapt old ways to those new needs. One of the singular strengths of Christianity as a religion has always been its stunning ability to adapt; and no historic Christians better exemplify that strength than John Wesley and his younger brother Charles.

5

Too Many Names for Sam

Every family has its usable problems, the totally minor and faintly annoying ones that are the very framework for holding life together, so to speak. It has long been my conviction that the major matters contribute almost nothing except to the family albums which no one ever looks at and everyone insists that Mother keep. Personally I have a huge chest and two steamer trunks full of major matters. They show every evidence of being about to degenerate into three bulky containers always in the way. At that point, I suppose, the chest and two trunks will be minor, and therefore structural, problems in and of themselves; but that's not the fundamental insight I had in mind to tell you about.

Our most minor and pervasive problem has always been too many Sams . . . or too many names for those we have. Husband Sam has never liked his name, and I think that that's where it really begins.

"Sam," fifty-odd years ago, was not a stylish southern name, and was always, as a result, getting lengthened or elaborated to something else . . . usually Sammy or Samuel or Sambo.

Sam grew up tolerating the lengthened forms, which

he hated, because the alternatives were worse . . . his middle name was Milton. Blind poets aside, there's very little one can do with Milton. It was a gift, before the fact, from his older sister.

There was a distant and adored uncle in Florida named Uncle Milton (one should note here that that sits rather well on the ear—maybe we should say that laying aside blind poets and distant uncles, there's very little one can do with Milton). Well, be that as it may, the point is that when sister Lee was five and Sam was on the way, she prayed for a baby brother whom she could name Milton after the hero uncle. When the birth occurred and events had indeed granted a male child, nothing would do but that he should be named Milton. To do otherwise, my mother-in-law used to tell me, would have been to shatter the child's faith too early. Sam always countered that shattered silliness is much to be desired in one's spiritual development; but by the time he was old enough to voice that opinion, it was too late. He had been firmly and immutably Samuel Milton Tickle for years.

My mother-in-law, stuck as she was with half a name for her final offspring, tried to counteract the puritan effect by choosing a vigorous, Old Testament name. Because she was a godly woman at an entirely believable level of everyday practice, I always believed her when she said that she had added Samuel to his name for Hannah's reasons; that she too had "asked him of the LORD" (1 Sam. 1:20). I used to love to hear her say his name: "Samuel! Samuel! Come here a minute!" I always heard Hannah's love and Hannah's voice somehow. Besides, being married to him, I was awfully glad for his sake that one of us could regard him as a gift from God.

Thus, in our early years as children growing up

together in the same neighborhood, we heard Mrs. Tickle say "Samuel"; we kids all said "Sam" or "Sambo"; and my father—God rest his soul—always said "Sammy." (His best friend in childhood had been named "Sammy," and he just couldn't seem to break the habit. It was a practice that did not make for postengagement happiness, but there it was and no help for it.)

The name problem was serious enough so that we were down to our sixth child (we stood at three girls and two boys already here) when I said, near the end of things, "If it's another boy, he's going to be Sam, Jr." Sam the Elder was as entrenched as ever . . . no more Samuels, no more Miltons, no juniors.

Of course the time of discovery came, and we did have another boy just as I had suspected. "Sam, Junior," I said, while still in Recovery. "John Wayne!" Sam snapped back.

The birth certificate lady came the next day while Sam, fortunately, was in absentia. Without the faintest qualm, I filled in the blank: Samuel Milton Tickle, Junior.

"You did what?"

"I named him Samuel Milton, Jr."

"I won't christen him that way!" But of course he did, since the days of two names—baptismal and legal—are long since gone. Right from the start, however, I knew we were in trouble. The older children tried "Sam" for about ten minutes after we got home from the hospital and then switched to "Milton."

"He looks so much like Daddy I feel disrespectful calling him the same name" was Mary's then-twelve-year-old explanation of the problem. But "Milton"? It had never occurred to me that we would call him Milton. Obviously the distant uncle had never been

61

enough of a favorite to command this kind of longevity. Nonetheless, Milton it was . . . for four years and kindergarten.

On our way in to register for kindergarten not a word was said. I filled in the registration card and then went back to underline, as instructed, "the name by which this child is called."

"Why'd you do that?"

"It says to underline the name we call you at home."

"No way, Jose!" was his response. He took my pen, wiggledy-lined out my mark, and underlined the "S–A–M" of his first name. "There!" he said.

Registration cards made no difference at home, of course. The children, Sam, and I still called him Milton . . . Mary was very right by then. The older he grew, the more like his father he became. Even I felt funny calling him Sam. I could remember when his father had looked exactly that way. There were—and are—times when he is working intently on a project in the shop or bending over his desk studying when I have a sense of shock that Sam's become immortal on this side of heaven—or that I have interrupted two lives, or one life twice, as the case may be.

Now, as his voice has deepened and so have those of his friends, when the phone is for Sam, it's anybody's guess who's calling whom. When his friends are over and I inadvertently call for Milton, it's still anybody's guess whom I'm calling . . . except for the guilty party and he refuses to answer. On a recent visit home, oldest sister Nora, listening to one such afternoon of confusion, suggested that maybe it was time to try Sambo again. Both father and brother nearly killed her. Mary backed them up, reiterating her longtime position that it didn't matter how many variations we invented for the name, the problem still was that the ectoplasm was absolutely identical.

I assume that, given the course of natural development, the problem will be limited in the next few years to family reunions and infrequent letters. I also assume that, even now while both men are still in the same house, the problem is no longer a working one anyway. The problem, as I said right from the beginning, is now absorbed into the structure of what we are. It's become one of those warp or weft threads that hold memories and relationships together. It's a little like the problem of Baptist, Methodist, and Catholic in the kingdom of God, I suspect. The ectoplasm is always the same regardless of the names. Besides, that's not just Mary's opinion; it seems to have been His also. What was it He said during their last times together? "A new commandment I give unto you, That ye love one another. . . . In my Father's house are many mansions: if it were not so, I would have told you" (John 13:34; 14:2). Well, something like that anyway.

Lent

The forty penitential weekdays and six festal Sundays that Mardi Gras opens the door for are the days of greatest calm in the church's year. Since by long centuries of custom the date of Easter is annually determined from the first Sunday after the full moon on or after March 21, the intertwining of physical and spiritual seasons is virtually inevitable. The resulting union of deep winter and holy preparation makes reflection, even penitence, a natural activity.

The denial of self and the giving up of favorite activities and foods are less followed now than in earlier centuries . . . or perhaps they are simply less loudly proclaimed by the participants. Certainly for most of us who keep the fast of Lent there has been considerable modification from the ways of the Renaissance church, the changes in diet being less dramatic and more intended to remind than to chastise. But however Lent is kept or used in contemporary Christendom, it is increasingly informed by the approaching Great Fifty Days of Easter, rather than itself informing them.

6

Final Sanity

Written originally during Lent 1980 when Rebecca was five and her brothers were eight and ten.

Last night there was a storm . . . a cold front shifting suddenly and dropping onto us with ferocity and winds that bent down the pine trees along the fence line. Sometime after I went to bed, it tore open the pasture gate; so we awoke this morning to bitter cold and a scattered herd. Two pregnant heifers in the front yard, six more in the garden eating up what was left of the turnip greens, and seven others, mostly yearlings, playing at some kind of heifer tag in the windy orchard.

The mud from last month's snow was three inches thick. Even frozen, it came laughing up to suck off our boots. We slopped and fell and prodded swollen bellies until, ourselves covered with ooze, we fell onto the broken gate and laughed our laugh to the gray dawn skies and the startled blackbirds. We drove the last ones through finally, my son and I, and repaired the gate right enough, coming in out of the cold with feet so wet and frozen that we couldn't feel them and with our nightclothes covered in the half-thawed manure. We stank up the kitchen with the good stench of late winter and of the earth when it is resisting one last cold front with the heat of coming fertility.

Later I stood at the spigot and washed the mud from our boots and felt again, as I do every year at this season, a grief for the passing cold. Looking across the pastures to the pond below, I knew it had indeed been the last storm before the spring, and I wanted to run backward toward the early morning, toward the winds and breaking limbs of last night.

"Lenzin," our German ancestors used to call this season, and since then we have called it "Lent." It is a time when Christians decorate stone churches with the sea's color and wrap their priests in the mollusk's purple. It was once a time when all things passed through the natural depression of seclusion, short food supplies, and inactivity, a time when body and land both rested. It is still, in the country, a final sanity before the absurd wastefulness of spring.

Each year at this time it is harder for me to desire butterflies and lilies, even to wish for resurrection. Each year I come a little closer to needing the dullness of the sky and the rarity of a single redheaded woodpecker knocking for grubs in my pine bark. Each year also I come a little closer to the single-mindedness of the drake who, muddy underside showing, waddles now across the ice to the cold center water to wash himself for his mate, all in the hope of ducklings later on.

Through the thin, sharp air I can hear the younger children in the barn. They are building tunnels again, making forts from the dried bales of hay. From the yapping I know that even the dogs can join in the intricacies which imagination has contrived. The five-year-old chases field mice as her brothers build. She will catch another soon and drown it in the water trough with unsullied sadism, feeling only the accomplishment that comes from having helped to keep her part of the world in balance.

In the summer, the mice will leave, going back to the fields again, and she will take to pulling everything that blooms instead, bringing them all in to me indiscriminately. The tin-roofed barn will be stifling, and the forts will have all been eaten. The boys will be picking beans and complaining of the itch from the okra leaves, being themselves too hot and tired to desire anything except nightfall and bed. The drake will have a family, which he will abandon to the mate he so much desires now, and the woodpecker's carmine head will burn out to tired tan. The farm in the summer becomes like the city is all year . . . too much color, too much noise, too much growing, too much hurry to stave off loss and destruction, too little natural death and gentle ending, too little time for play, too little pointless imagination.

I can remember many summers now; it is the singular advantage of years that one can do so. And I remember that once summer comes, I spend it wallowing in the easiness of it; the excess of its fruits and vegetables, the companionship of its constant sounds as the hum of the insects and of the Rototillers gives way in the evening to the croaking of the frogs and the raucousness of the katydids. I remember also that I begin early, in that green time of Trinity, to dread the stillness of the coming cold; to fear the weariness of winter menus, the bitterness of breaking open pond water for thirsty cattle and of packing lunches—interminable lunches—for reluctant children on their way to school.

But for right now it is Lent and for one more snow I can luxuriate in the isolation of the cold, attend laconically to who I am and what I value and why I'm here. Religion has always kept earth time. Liturgy only gives sanction to what the heart already knows.

March 25—The Annunciation

The several seasons we call "Easter" are by far the most concentrated in the liturgical calendar, which is a way of saying that they are the most clearly defined and directed. Only five saints are remarked during the ninety-seven days, and only one non-Easter event—the Annunication.

Long celebrated by the church and never a victim of the contention between Protestant and Roman views of the faith, the Annunciation has enjoyed a kind of quiet presence in many branches of Christianity. So easy, in fact, has been its life as a holy day that it has suffered somewhat in import. Yet, for women in particular, it is an ironic juxtaposition that the woman of the Pieta was first the girl of the Annunciation. Not a one of us but understands that irony. Not a one of us but should hand it on to her children.

7

On Just Such a Morning

There are no walls to experience, the farm inside me being always larger and freer than the one which lies waiting outside my kitchen window. I am my own window this morning, and I come to my prayers like Janus looking both ways . . . outward to where Nimrod the mighty stalks the patio in pursuit of a guinea chick he doesn't really want, and inward to where a thousand equally casual deaths and near deaths have blended into acceptance and peace in the balance.

Dublin the rooster stands tall on the gatepost of the chicken yard. During the winter that preceded us, he lost his comb to the bitter cold, having preferred the pain of frostbite to confinement in the hen house. Now, crownless except for his scar of black and withered skin, he sways from his perch more vigorously than he did when he was whole. This too I bring in to me, this regard for scars and purchase.

The early spring crowds around us—around Dublin and Nimrod and me. It waddles with the ducks crossing the greening yard toward the fowl lot and scurries with the guineas in their frantic discovery of the missing chick. It grows deeply and insistently up the kitchen window toward me, vining and budding as it comes;

but I am having none of it. I'll not be so easy a convert to merriment this morning. Too many beginning springs have seduced me before this one.

Beyond the fence line Flash, the gelding, moves away from the mares to look across the yard, an immense air of tragedy pervading the whole of him. He stops briefly to neigh toward the kitchen door, lowers his head to scratch his neck along the cedar railing, and moves on. He has no prayers standing between him and his ordinary habits—no interior pasture in which to feed—and I am glad for the simpleness of his purpose, the directness of his life. Mine is not so—certainly not this morning, when I walk two lands, the one which I house having been built of daily pieces from the one in which I am myself housed.

It must have been on just such a morning as this that the young Mary first was told, first knew that she stood between two worlds . . . and "she was troubled at his saying" (Luke 1:29) . . . and across the intervening centuries I reach out to her fear and reverence her confusion.

Below me on the patio Nimrod tries again for the chick, but this time the cock is there. It is over in less time than it takes me to laugh—the cock on the cat; talons burying deep in fur; beak pecking hair and drawing blood; fur and feathers intertwined and racing across the patio and into the low-lying holly bushes; Nimrod, scraped free of his burden by the low-lying prickles; and the guineas on guinea patrol around the bed. Even Flash has turned back to watch, and Dublin, ever a gossip, crows his delight from atop the hen house roof.

It's all too much for me, and I am at last seduced. I go out into the farmyard, adding, as I go, its frolic to my prayers. Of these things, too, is worship made.

Holy Week

Holy Week begins with what used to be simply known as "Palm Sunday" and now is also sometimes referred to as "Passion Sunday" because the record of Our Lord's passion is always read from pulpits across the world on this last Sunday before Easter. It is still, nonetheless, the palms themselves that mark the day for most of us . . . the blaring of the trumpets . . . the anthems of Hosanna . . . the triumph of procession. They will all be followed much too quickly, however, by Maundy Thursday, Good Friday, and Holy Saturday, by the most solemn and depressed days of the Christian year.

In our country parish the Maundy Thursday service is almost as well attended as is the Easter service itself. We gather together in communion to celebrate again the Last Supper held on this night so many centuries ago. Then, sitting in the darkened nave, the benediction having been said, and the choir having recessed, we watch from the pews as the women of the parish strip away—vessel by vessel and candlestick by candlestick—every trapping and utensil of the faith until, faced with a naked altar and a barren chancel, the priest himself begins the washing of the holy place.

There will be no communion here these next two days, no giving of wine and bread. The giver is dead.

On Good Friday from high noon to midafternoon, during the final three hours of His passion, the choir will chant quietly, and the men will read aloud from the lectern beside that stark altar as we of the laity come and go, praying from our places in the pews. It is a somber remembrance of humiliation willingly assumed, of pain which lies beyond telling, of penetration into truth through agony. Those who have not passed through Holy Week never arrive at the Eastertide which ends it.

8

The Old Priest Grinning

Last fall I attended an adult baptism. If I had known that there was to be a baptism, I would not even have gone to church.

Becca was nursing the last of a virus and sleeping late that morning. Sam and the boys were converting the garage into an office for me.

They had worked half the night before and had been up since daylight again, trying to finish the outside work before the cold set in. I already felt guilty about leaving them and her, but it was Sunday. I had no ox in the ditch, and habit took over. So there I was, trapped in a morning eucharist which was totally centered—propers, collects, and all—toward an adult baptism.

The adult involved was a young woman I had never seen before that day, but she was hugely pregnant . . . so near to birthing that she could scarcely bend over the font for the actual baptizing, much less kneel afterward for the elements. As I watched the service, I wondered with sincere dread and an icy stomach what had led her to this decision at this point in her life. Why not wait until after her child was born? Why do so private a thing in public, especially now?

One part of the regular Episcopal eucharist that I

routinely dislike is the passing of the peace. Some priest intones, "The peace of God be always with you," and we respond from the pews, "And also with you," and everyone shakes hands with each other as if with strangers. Acolytes shake hands with the lay readers with whom they, not twenty minutes ago, were rehearsing the order of the service, including this very part. The members of the congregation turn in the pews to shake hands with the folk they were just arguing town politics with in the narthex before services. It is so artificial that I can hardly bear to watch it, and I have for years adamantly refused to do it.

Unfortunately, the service of baptism is even worse than the regular eucharist, at least in Episcopalianism. Not only do we seem to pass the peace interminably during the service (an exaggeration, you understand), but we also renew our own vows after the convert makes his or hers.

Question: Do you renounce Satan and all the spiritual forces of wickedness that rebel against God?

Answer: I renounce them.

Question: Do you renounce the evil powers of this world which corrupt and destroy the creatures of God?

Answer: I renounce them.

Question: Do you renounce all sinful desires that draw you from the love of God?

Answer: I renounce them.

Question: Do you turn to Jesus Christ and accept him as your Savior?

Answer: I do.

Question: Do you put your whole trust in his grace and love?

Answer: I do.

Question: Do you promise to follow and obey him as
  your Lord?
Answer: I do.

I am uncomfortable with such talk for adults. With
children it seems all right. Such words are, if not appropriate, then at least less embarrassing, to children. (It
was, in fact, more the age than the stressed condition of
the candidate that bothered me, I decided.)

Then the water in the font had to be blessed. Once
blessed it had to be cupped over the head of the woman,
and the words of the baptism spoken. Then there was
the welcoming . . . "We receive you into the household
of God. Confess the faith of Christ crucified, proclaim
his resurrection, and share with us in his eternal
priesthood." And, of course, the peace was passed.

I had not seen an adult baptism in years, for they are
more usually done privately with only the convert's
sponsors. But by this point I felt I had seen every piece
of paganism and indignity I could tolerate in this one.
My repugnance was so total that I could hardly stand
still in the pew . . . until I looked sideways across the
aisle at the town librarian. Unless his face was lying, his
anguish was as great as my own. I peeked up out of
lowered eyes to the choir in front of us. Almost to a
person they, too, looked distressed, their eyes lowered, I
thought, out of more than reverence. Then I outright
raised my head and began to assess all of us. As I stood
up straighter, the celebrating priest, over all those
bowed heads, caught my eye, grinned, and nodded.

He was an old gentleman—very old, in fact. Our
parish had been without a regular priest for six months
because the bishop had urged our pastor to a less rural
parish without remembering to have a replacement
handily up his cassock sleeve. A new rector was coming

in November, and we were all relieved. But the old priest had become something of a fixture over the summer months, and I was already suspecting that we would miss him. When he grinned, I was very sure I was going to.

As I passed through the nave doors into the narthex after the service, I shook his hand, as everyone always does after the services. As we shook, he whispered to me, "Bothers you, does it?"

"A lot," I answered.

"Good," he said. "You remember that next Lent when I'm gone."

Well, that was October, and this is April. Just as the old priest said, it is Lent and he is gone. I have seen the young woman off and on all the fall and winter. Her baby—a boy—was baptized after church one day last December. I stayed to watch as did most of the parish. It was a simple, easy service, one that had most of us crying, in no way harsh like her own had been, and my emotions were in no way reminiscent of those on the stressful Sunday of her vows.

Now it is Holy Week—her first as a Christian, and my own who-knows-how-manyeth? Yet every time I look at that young woman or her baby, I see the librarian, who has since moved on to a bigger system and a better job; or I think of the old priest who has returned undisturbed to his retirement. Only his admonition that I should remember still sticks in my head.

I don't want to remember. It offends me as much now as it did on that October day to know that we are just human and supposed to be; that there's some duality I can't accept but which we must call "Satan" because he is there; that half the words of the liturgy are not directed toward divinity but toward our union with each other; and—ultimate irony—that it takes theater to connect us to process because we can't yet connect to what we can't feel.

O God, I think. *How I hate the road to Calvary! If you'd only been more godly, we could have both been spared this agony!*

Suddenly it's already Easter in my heart, and I want to laugh out loud—I know why the old priest grinned!

Easter

Death, I am told, fascinates poets; and since, technically anyway, I am one of those, I suppose I am fascinated—or else, ought to be. Certainly it is much easier to write about death than about life, mainly because we are all drawn to it like the proverbial moth to his candle.

It is all the things that mythographers and poets have invented from time immemorial to convey its mystery . . . it is Pandora's box that must not be opened. It is the world on the other side. It is God.

Yet I suppose that never and nowhere is it accepted for long as the end. As a finality, Christian faith certainly never gives a distinctive geography to death, but it shares with many faiths its recognition that a geography does exist.

9

Of This April's Showers

First published for Easter 1984 when Rebecca was nine and her brothers twelve and fourteen.

Along the edge of the front walkway and just to the inside of the curve where the flagstones turn to follow the line of the house, Sam has planted a row of hyacinths. They are, admittedly, not much as today's hyacinths go; a long way removed, in fact, from the lush Dutch imports in the yards and flower beds of most of our city friends. Each March and April they bloom up shorter and more timid of color than most, and with blooms which only sparsely decorate the hesitant spikes from which they depend. But it is not for their flowerness that we have them.

They are Great-great-grandmother Gammon's hyacinth bulbs. Over a century and a half ago she fetched them from Virginia to the Appalachian foothills in her own migration westward. Since then each Gammon child has fetched them again as he or she left the homeplace to push further on. For all we know, the bulbs may have originally been brought by the family from the other side of the Atlantic. About that the family records are vague; but we are very sure of the last hundred and fifty years and of the genealogy of the bulbs in this country.

Apparently Sam, in carrying the bulbs all the way to the Mississippi River, has brought them farther west than have any other of Great-great-grandmother's descendants. He has, in keeping with family tradition, planted them inside the walkway curves of five houses and has four times dug them up again to make yet another move with us. And each time an older child has moved away from our house—or from any other in the family, for that matter—a clump of those special hyacinths has left in the moving van with him or her. So Great-great-grandmother's hyacinths bloom in dozens of yards each spring, making a chain of connection across the southern United States and more than one hundred fifty years.

What blooms every spring also, of course, is an understanding of what mattered in 1825. In a hard land with its scarcity of domesticated flowers, Great-great-grandmother must have seen in the hyacinths a portable symbol of her eventual victory over a wilderness . . . and enough promise of future generations so she built and passed on emphatically the ritual of the hyacinth.

There may also have been more to it than that. When I was a child growing up in the mountains of East Tennessee, the world seemed to me to be an insurmountable garden in which I was at best only a visitor passing through. The trees and the plants were pieces of the earth which rose and sank with the seasons and with the courses of their own life cycles; but they were the earth while I was only on it. It was a distinction that made the trees, in particular, seem to be more powerful and more ominous than any other part of my daily surroundings. They towered over everything we did. It was as if they were only waiting for us to grow weary or leave so that they could, with their shade and leaves and falling limbs and spreading roots, consume for the earth all that we had temporarily effected on the surface.

I was never much of a flower lover, even in those days of childhood—at least not a grower and cutter of flowers. My joy was all in the open fields and hillsides where the flowers bloomed rampant and uncontrolled in the silly profusion of daisies and brown-eyed Susies. It was the Dutchman's breeches and the jack-in-the-pulpits hiding beside the wild mountain streams that gave me pleasure. My father's yard and those of our neighbors seemed then (and still seem) to be only extensions of their houses . . . like rooms created outside of walls instead of within them, rooms in which the furnishings are constantly being refurbished by planning and unrelenting care. Since every season I knew the earth was going to win again by taking back to herself what my father and our neighbors had so painfully put there, the yards appeared to me as no more than exercises in human ego. They appeared to grow from human need to impose human will, however briefly, on the earth, in full knowledge that we could never hold off the natural chaos of vegetable life for long; that we could never stop the preordained pattern of rebirth from dead forms.

So with the ignorance of a child I met the trees, plants, and flowers as creatures whose life purposes and cycles were superior to my own by virtue of their indestructibility and total mutability. What bloomed today as a daisy would bloom next year as a sunflower or a hollyhock. And I knew them all in the intimate way of children. I found the king in the pansy bloom and learned to make the morning glories cry out. I popped the Japanese lanterns and made shakers from the poppy pods. But mainly I dealt carefully with them all. They were not my friends. They were mysteries sent upon the earth as tokens, evidence of the need for caution, warnings to never forget that I was not of them.

It was natural to me, then, in my eighth year, when I discovered the ancient Greek legends, to understand the reverence from which the myths had sprung. What my elders called ignorance or superstition I saw as irrefutable and solid explanation. I wandered in my ninth year through a world of gods and demigods whom my father pruned, but whom I knew he would never discipline or shape completely to his will . . . whom I knew neither of us would outlive. It was a great joke I shared with the goldenrod and the pussy willow that they would live forever and we would not. The fact that Christianity later soaked through my understanding and forced me to change my notions of relative immortality never affected my love for the mystery of the myths, especially not the mystery of the hyacinth.

A most grand German lady, who had known my family before World War II, had given me a copy of *The Wonderbook*. Leatherbound on deep boards and tooled by hand with gold letters and with a gold Pegasus emblazoned across it, it was a treasure trove of impossible glories, the noblest of which were the myths of the plant world. And there I met Hyacinthus, the beautiful young mortal who was loved by the god Apollo. But Hyacinthus was mortally wounded one day by a discus thrown by Apollo, and Apollo, knowing full well that creatures could never be immortal, could not save him. Instead the god quickly gathered each drop of blood as it fell from the boy's wound and planted the drops, one by one, in the soil of the playing court. From each drop of planted blood Apollo caused a flower to bloom, a bloom which on each of its spikes recounts the drops of blood Hyacinthus shed and Apollo garnered.

As Hyacinthus lay dying, the *Wonderbook* said, he uttered the mournful cry of universal human suffering,

the high-pitched wailing lament of the dying . . .
Ai–Ai–Ai–Ai . . . across the hills and valleys of Hellas.
And as the blood of the slain boy bloomed, it bore in
itself the written symbols of his dying sounds. For all
the eternity which his flower life gave him, Hyacinthus
would continue to spell with his petals the *A* and the *I*
of his death cry. When I was eight, I didn't have to look
at a hyacinth to know that every word of the story was
absolutely true and that the strange two-petals-one-
petal-two-petals-one-petal arrangement of each individual blossom spelled *Ai–Ai–Ai–Ai*.

All of which should get us back to our front yard and
the bed that runs across it toward the drive and inside
the curve of the sidewalk. But early last February a
neighboring farmer lost some of his shoats, or young
hogs. They rooted out from under his fence, as un-
ringed shoats will do, and appeared in strange places.
One morning we woke up to a pond dam covered in
Poland China shoats. One morning our near neighbors
awoke to Polands in the barn. One afternoon, while we
were driving around the bend where the graveyard
meets our property line, we almost had a sausage accident. But there was no catching them. Then, a week or
so later, I came home at the end of a tedious day in town
to find three black-and-white Poland Chinas in the
front flower bed, rooting and grunting away. Hyacinths
have almost no nutritive value, but an absolutely delicious taste. Cows have been known to drown trying to
reach just a few more of the water variety, and pigs have
an insatiable appetite for the earthbound ones. I knew,
even before I had time to think it through, what had
happened. I grabbed a stick and a son, and we set to.
Never before in history have piglets suffered so much at
the hands of so few. We stood them off for an hour and
a half before Sam got home, and he and the owner
recaptured them at last. But the damage was unques-

tionably done. The whole bed was a mud bath of turned soil and pig tracks mixed with frayed sticks and a little blood. The younger children were solemn afterward, sobered by some sense of failure which they could not quite identify or define. Sam's distress was contagious. He knew clearly what had been violated. For days he left each morning by the front door, stood briefly in front of the trampled bed, sighed, and moved on to the car. The earth had defeated at least his small part of Great-great-grandmother's plan. It had simply reclaimed its own, despite five human generations. The century and a half that were success to us were nothing to the earth, and her patience had been as infinite as her victory.

Yet the unlikely and presumably impossible happened. It was on the rainiest day of this singularly rainy April when we found them . . . three stalks, shorter than most and more timid of color, the blooms only sparsely covering the spikes from which they depended, but they were there . . . three of them, a clump for each of the children who has yet to grow up and leave home. Rebecca, who at eight going on nine has grown up with a head full of Greek legends and family stories, pulled a bloom off—a single bloom—and set it on the supper table in a little dish of water. And across the fields of Lucy Goosey Farm its six petals . . . two-petals-one-petal-two-petals-one-petal . . . spelled *Ai-Ai-Ai* in the yellow light of the setting sun. This Sunday, as he does every year on Easter, our priest will again cry out from the pulpit, "Death, where is thy victory?" But this year for the first time Rebecca will understand that at least the beginning of the answer to his question lies somewhere between Great-great-grandmother Gammon's picture on the front room wall and Mount Olympus. It has been her first lesson in serious religion.

The Great Fifty Days

The Great Fifty Days are the center of the church's year. It is here within these seven weeks that we celebrate by name and in detail all that Easter has made possible.

If Easter is resurrection, then the Great Fifty Days direct our attention to what that resurrection means. They celebrate, in particular, the presence of a risen God active in human life through an indwelling Spirit and active in divine life through an ascended Son. They speak to the high priesthood of that Son, to his guardianship and his protectorship. They speak to the inviolate union of the faithful with one another in the communion of shared body and blood. They speak, always and most directly, to life without ending. Such realities are more a source of awe than of mere happiness, and their celebration more an ecstasy than a time.

10

Father and Son

We are talking in the kitchen. It is Saturday just before lunch, and my hands are busy the way they always are when I am in the kitchen. It is this busyness of hands in peeling and cutting and washing that buys children time for talk, and it is easy talk today. He is sitting on the kitchen counter, all six feet of him dangling and hanging with the same nonchalance of fifteen years ago when I first showed him how to sit here and hold on without falling. The counter top even has a crack now in the front edge where his increasing weight has pulled it loose. I feel obliged from time to time to fuss at him for the crack that means Sam will someday have to replace the counter, but he only says, "Aw, Maw!" knowing I treasure the cracked counter far too much to lose it for the sake of a more attractive one.

He kicks the cabinet doors with the heels of his tennis shoes, swinging his legs and stretching that incredible leanness of his. He knows he is beautiful, a Greek god come to a Tennessee farm, and he plays his advantage as expertly as his baby sister plays hers with his father. He talks about the car he's going to buy next summer as soon as he has made enough money. He rambles about the job he wants hanging sheet rock

93

with a construction firm, and I remind him that he is the laziest child we have. I also remind him that his father is at this very moment building shelves in the shop, an endeavor with which he could probably be of substantial help. He knows I don't mean that either, and doesn't bother to answer . . . only grins. He'd slipped away from the shop and into the kitchen ten minutes ago to have this time over the potatoes, and he intends to have it. He raises one leg laconically and sets his heel on the sink rim. I thrust my paring knife at his shoe, but it bothers him not at all. He grins again, and the talk of cars becomes a kind of soft rumble in which I am carried more by the music of his deepening voice than by his content.

Suddenly, without any preliminary break in his monologue, he vaults off the corner of the counter and throws himself half across the kitchen. Taking the steps three at a time, he is down to his room and back again. He races by me and out the kitchen door. I hear the gun before I can even guess what he's about. Above the report of the second shot I hear the yelp of the dog and the barking of its companion. I see him running fast, gun at the ready, across the yard, vaulting the fence and into the fields. I watch as he draws, and the cry of the second dog comes back to me before the report does. The guineas suddenly find their voices and frantically begin their screaming from the high pines where they had apparently fled.

He crosses the fence back toward me, and I see him eject the unspent shells as he comes.

"Got 'em both!" he slams the back door and sets the gun beside it. "I can hear the others over toward Austins' and in the cemetery."

The wild dogs that roam the river bottoms are a greater threat to us than any other predator, especially in the spring when the river rises and drives them in to us. Mainly they want the calves. It is rare for them to come up so near the house.

"I didn't even see them," I say.

"Saw 'em out of the corner of my eye when the guineas flew up," he responds, settling back on to the counter, wedging his back again into the corner of the overhanging cabinets. He is as relaxed and placid as he was ten minutes ago before it all began.

"You'd better clean the gun."

"Not yet. The others will be back to eat these. I'll try to get 'em then." He slides off the counter, our conversation apparently over, and heads back to the shop to help with the shelves.

I can't remember when or how it began, this easiness of warfare in him. I can remember in the second year of our being here that the coyotes came in from the bottoms, and Sam spent every night for a week hiding in the loft of the barn before he finally managed to kill some and drive the rest of the pack away. But this one was an infant then, a darling little package of blond good looks still going to grade school in the mornings and bringing me pictures for the refrigerator door in the afternoons. I remember that he was only mildly curious about what his father was doing in the barn every night. I do recall the morning he came upstairs and, half asleep still, told me, "Daddy got one last night. I heard it yelp," but I never thought of it as more than a child talking about his nighttime.

Maybe his father taught him to shoot without my knowing that that was what they were about. There are the bitter cold nights every winter when the possums come to steal the cat food and warm themselves inside the patio wall. We will hear the kittens cry or the pans rattle against the ice, and one of them, father or son, will get the gun. My chest will hold my breath tightly until the retort is over, and I know once more there has been no ricochet. What I can't remember was when it was, at what point in our lives, that Sam quit going out with him, or even going at all. When did they, and by what agreement between them, pass the killing on to him?

Perhaps it was that night in the hen house two years ago. Bitter cold at midnight when the hens began to scream. They both went, I remember, a gun with each of them, and me trailing behind. I got to the gate of the hen yard just in time to hear Sam shout, "Now! Shoot now!" and to hear the gun.

Inside and muffled I heard his voice, "You OK?"

"Yeah. Thanks, Son. He got my sleeve before I saw him." Then, "You're a pretty good marksman in the dark."

"I could see his tail flick. How many chickens did he get?"

"Only two. We can throw them out tomorrow when it's light."

"OK." And they came out.

Not a word was ever said to me except by Sam, in passing, "Lost two this time. No way in the world to keep coons out."

Later I found the slash in his jacket sleeve and the tear where the coon was clinging when the boy dropped him. Yes, maybe that was the night. I never thought of it till now. But after that the guns moved one by one down to his bedroom, supposedly so he could keep them oiled and maintained. Even Papaw's ancient rifle went down. I should have known that that was what was happening, that guardianship was moving to the boy.

They both come in the side door together, the smell of the potatoes and my new peas having made its way even to the shop. He's saying, "I probably oughta go down there by the cemetery after lunch and see if they're still there . . . probably be easier to get 'em there than

96

up in the field. These two looked like they were half coyote. If so, they'll run tonight unless I can get them."

"Let's eat first." And they begin washing at the sink.

He eats as completely and as loosely as he does everything else, no hurry apparent in his motions, but long before we are done, he nods his own dismissal and is gone out the door, the gun once more in his hand. I remark how naturally it sits there, how matter-of-factly he handles it.

"Of course. What else did you expect? He's a boy."

"Doesn't it ever worry you that he kills so quickly?"

"No, only that he might not kill quickly enough. I've seen what a dog can do. He never has."

"He saw you the night the coon got your arm."

He looks up, startled that I know. "You never miss a trick, do you?"

"Somebody had to mend your jacket."

"Well, I'm glad he saw it . . . better my jacket than his hand someday."

Far off to th east of the house I hear the gun. "Maybe he got one," I say.

"Maybe. Be glad when he's back."

"It does worry you!" I am triumphant at this break in male indifference.

"It should always worry you to send a son against a natural enemy if you've got good sense." He is exasperated with me. "But it'd be a lot worse if he weren't there to send." And he is gone back to his making and building.

It is not, I think as he leaves, *the worst set of thoughts with which to end the first week of the Great Fifty Days.*

April 25—St. Mark

St. Mark's Day always sticks in my head because of a fluke, a situation which is a bit unfair to poor St. Mark.

Certainly St. Mark has played a rather substantial role in Christian history, particularly in his writing of the earliest Gospel which bears his name and from which the other three to some extent derived.

Certainly he is impressively commemorated across the world by massive architectural wonders that bear his name and do him homage.

Certainly, as a child, I was charmed completely by the story of his near arrest in the Garden of Gethsemane. Supposedly Mark was the youth whose tunic was ripped off by the arresting soldiers, and he fled the Garden naked. When one is a child, stories of nakedness in anyone titillate, and even more so in a saint. Besides, it seemed to me then to have been a better excuse for abandoning the Garden than was enjoyed by the rest of the Apostles. (In fact, it still comes very close in my mind to being an explanation as well as a pretty sound reason for leaving!) None of these things, however, is why I always remember St. Mark's Day.

Because Easter—or the date for Easter, more correctly—always fluctuates in accord with the date of the first full moon after March 21, it will never fall on the same day in any two consecutive years. Yet the range within which it can come—the earliest possible date and the latest—is fixed forever by that equinox. And Easter can never be later than April 25! St. Mark's Day is Easter's last chance.

As a youngster I somehow convinced myself that the twenty-fifth was called "St. Mark's Day" because it "marked" the last possible date for Easter . . . and because those in the ancient church were always fond of having fun with things like that. Years of living have not appreciably changed my suspicions, at least not about the church fathers; but they have changed my perception of what St. Mark's marks. St. Mark's Day means the final and irrefutable death of winter for yet another year.

$\boxed{11}$

Through the Veil Torn

The spring comes so quietly in the country, so without announcement, that I walk into it morning after morning without knowing until abruptly, on some perfectly ordinary day, I think, *It's warm!* and realize that I have already been jacketless and easy in my kingdom for several such mornings. Faith is a bit like that, I suspect, quiet and without announcement, till it too seeps into our clothing and our decisions and only at the last into our consciousness, till it too cuts us loose from chores and clothes and awkwardness of foot.

My joy, of course, is in my freedom. The animals are with us again, or I am with them. The fence line no longer holds me separate. I move into their pastures, walking among them as they graze; or they join me in my ramblings down to the pond or off to the close. The world under our feet and about our faces and above our heads is alive again with bees and moths and butterflies and grasshoppers and dragonflies and ladybugs and a myriad such lives. Their energy charms me, but it is their variety—more infinite than that of the stars—which could beguile me.

It would be so easy, walking these acres, sharing this space, to grow placid and fat of soul—to love these creatures and their haunts beyond their function and place. So beautiful they are to me that only a cross keeps me from the metaphor of pantheism . . .

A cross, a Book, and an other who, because of them, lives so close now that I have lost our borders as well as our beginnings. And each Eastertide our conversation is laid aside more completely, more readily, than in the previous spring, while what has been in history and what is always being in nature blend into the sureness that contains both.

May 1—St. Philip and St. James

Since I was named for my father, whose given name was Philip, I can only claim St. Philip's as my patronal day, once removed. The once removed has never bothered me as much, however, as having to share the day with all the world's Jameses. Everybody should be entitled to one patronal day unshared, or so it seems to me.

These inconveniences are more than compensated for, however, by the rewards of having saints' days in general and one—or even a piece of one—assigned to oneself as a particular day for remembering.

12

Patronal Day

In the years of my early schooling during and just after the Second World War, we children were required to read, from time to time, sections of Butler's *Lives of the Principal Saints* for our literature or social studies classes. It was an assignment I always stoutly refused to honor. My father was deathly afraid of "all things papist," as he so charmingly put it; and I was deathly afraid of reading about things that were physically painful. Between the two of us, therefore, we managed to give me more than enough reason to steer wide of any talk of—or reading about—sanctified pain, and I graduated from high school and later from college without ever once having opened Butler. It was probably one of my more costly mistakes.

As a result of it—at least in part—I was still ill-prepared many years later for dealing with what was to happen to Sam and me. At two weeks of age, our second son and fifth child died of pneumonia.

Months after the violent passing, still numb and purposeless, we left the other children with our mothers and went off together on a kind of winter retreat or sabbatical in the mountains, hoping to discover there the energy and the perspective that would let us begin again.

It was the third or fourth day of our time there, and I was feeling more at peace than I had for weeks. The afternoon itself was cozily damp, and the mountains around us were glorious in their fog and drizzle. The secondhand bookstore where we were browsing was charming and quiet. A teakettle, if you can believe it, even simmered on the potbellied stove in the back. The whole village, in fact, was straight out of a brochure, but I was greatly in need of clichés. I was even beginning to trust them. Then suddenly, there on the shelf in front of me, was Butler—a bit mildewed, but there. Invulnerable at last, or so I thought, I picked him up and began to read.

I had always known that whatever else saints may be about, they are most certainly about suffering. What I had never known is that saints are those who neither need their pain nor value it nor ask anything of it. Butler's saints asked of misfortune no cosmic meaning and no personal gain. Indeed, as I stood there reading page after page, it was not the denial of pleasure or the pursuit of poverty or the desire for martyrdom (which things I had always assumed marked a saint), but the letting go which seemed to characterize Butler's heroes. It was, as a discovery, a great shock to my new equilibrium, one I deeply resented at the time.

There is in real pain, I had discovered, and in genuine grief, a kind of immunity from more pain or even from much engagement. Having suffered, I felt that I would not have to suffer again for a long, long time—perhaps even for the rest of my life. I had bought my peace the hard way. Even more, because I had hurt and still was hurting, I knew I was alive. I could touch that pain and be reassured by it, could flatter myself that it had some meaning beyond bacteria and medical accident. I even dredged up Aeschylus and persuaded myself that I had indeed gained wisdom through all of this . . . after all, these were the insights which our friends and family had sent us to the mountains to achieve.

But there was Butler with his tales of men and women who didn't have to hold on to their pain; who didn't need it to buy themselves immunity from life; who didn't find the reassurance of their own worth in it. Why? Butler seemed to be saying that it was because they every one—to a man and to a woman—believed themselves to have already been validated by God's pain; they believed that all those things I was asking of my grief had already been provided by divine grief. They had let go. I could not let go. It was the first time I had ever understood the necessity for his "Eloi, Eloi, lama sabachthani?"

I put Butler back on the shelf and left the store. It was only ten minutes later, back in our room, that I realized I had also left Sam, but it didn't matter. He took my absentmindedness as a sure sign of returning health, for absentmindedness has always characterized me as surely as better qualities have characterized the saints.

We left the next day. I couldn't bear all that pseudo-Tyrolean resort decor and said so rather forcefully. Sam laughed. It was the first time, I realized, that I had heard him laugh in weeks.

We came back to our lives and our children. In time we found the farm, bought it, and moved here. The ache for the boy who never grew up on it is no bigger and no smaller than it was all those years ago, just quieter and less arrogant—which is as much as any of us has any right to hope for from stories of other people's faith . . . at least in the beginning.

Rogation Days

Rogation Days were originally so named because they were the three days in which a completely rural Christendom asked . . . even begged . . . the blessing of God upon the earth and its crops. Now, removed as we are from any intimacy with the production of our food, we no longer feel the ancient urgency to *rogare*, as the Latin had it, "to ask or beseech."

We assume our food to be more threatened by teamsters' strikes than by bad weather, a change in perception which may speak more to our ingratitude than to our acumen. Yet despite the shifts in our understandings and customs, Rogation Days have stayed on many church calendars, laity and clergy alike being somehow reluctant to abandon them.

The days fall on the Monday, Tuesday, and Wednesday immediately preceding Ascension. Since the Thursday of Ascension is numbered from Easter and since Easter is calculated from the vernal equinox, the Rogation Days float, within a limited range of possibilities, with the natural calendar. They almost always, therefore, occur close to, or simultaneous with, that one part of life on our farm which invariably commands my attention—the coming of the fireflies.

The choice of scripture readings for the days of Rogation reflects graphically the shifting perception and definition of what modern believers want out of spring prayers. In earlier centuries the readings were drawn from those parts of the Old Testament which speak to the land flowing with milk and honey, to the land of easy tillage and gargantuan abundance. Now the propers tend to speak more to the wonder of the earth observed, to springtime and harvest, winter and rest as revelations of God. Particularly they draw from the Book of Job and from his experience with the whirlwind. The closing chapters of Job, likewise, have always commanded my attention—and my awe.

13

Dance of the Fireflies

The night when the fireflies mate is preceded by hours of subtle but obvious preparation. Regardless of how the day itself may have begun, the afternoon always moves with an unsettling orderliness. Even if a faint breeze plays about, no real wind disturbs the waiting grasses. Across the fence line and in the meadow the assertive green of middle spring changes to a yellow glow under an afternoon sun which invariably is warm but not yet hot. The cows, with a delicacy beyond my understanding, retreat before their usual hour to the feeding lot outside the barn. It is their early going, in fact, which most persuades me that this is the first of the three nights. Even the children will ask, "Is it time?" the quiet is so soft.

The dark comes late in the first days of May. And it comes luminous, like the world of my prayers where no thing is, save "is" itself. The meadow begins to grow indistinct and distant from the kitchen window. I step to the back door and see the first one. It is time.

In a family of many, most things are communal. This one is not. Whether they watch from other places on the farm, have other secret windows of their own, I don't know. I have never asked and never been told. I watch from just inside the fence line, sometimes sitting on a stump there, sometimes standing, sometimes resting in the hammock. Wherever I am, I will soon forget what and how.

The number of the lights increases slowly, a few here near me, a few over toward Mary's Hill. Rising from the meadow grasses they come in twos and threes and fours. By ten o'clock the meadow as far as I can see is filled with them, the air above the grasses flashing and throbbing with the dance of their passion.

By midnight they are all done. The blanket of lights settles gradually into the grass and finally stops altogether. Tomorrow night and the night after that they will mate again, but I will not come. Or coming, I will bring a child with me, and we will lean on the fence rail, chatting as we watch, like spectators at a zoo. Once the process has begun, once this copulation for which there is no perceptible schedule but in which all of nature seems to acquiesce, once this is in place, then it becomes indeed just another phenomenon to be remarked. It is only on this first night of confirmation that the awe hovers, like the lights of the dancing, about me.

The ancient story says that Job bowed down before the whirlwind and out of it heard the voice of his God.

Where wast thou when I laid the foundations of the earth? Declare, if thou hast understanding. . . . who laid the corner stone thereof; when the morning stars sang together, and all the sons of God shouted for joy? Or who shut up the sea with doors, when it brake forth, as if it had issued out of the womb? . . . Hast thou entered into the springs of the sea? Or hast thou walked in search of the depth? Have the gates of death been opened unto thee? Or hast thou seen the doors of the shadow of death? . . . Declare if thou knowest it all (Job 38:4–8; 16–18).

The story also says that Job, having heard, answered: "I have heard of thee by the hearing of the ear; but now mine eye seeth thee: wherefore I abhor myself, and repent in dust and ashes" (Job 42:5–6).

And, alone on this first night, caught in the whirlwind of their lights, I know that Job's story is true.

Ascension Day

The church has seven so-called Principal Feasts, days which are central to the liturgy because the events they remark are central to the faith. The seven are also days when the faithful, regardless of how we may slip and slide at other times, are expected to be in church at the time of the announced services. Three of the Principals fall within Christmas; three fall within Easter; the last marks the beginning of Ordinary Time.

Of the three Principals which Christians observe within the Great Fifty Days—Easter, Ascension, and Pentecost—Ascension is probably in the greatest danger of erosion. It always falls on the Thursday before Pentecost, and a weekday service is admittedly more difficult for the modern family to attend. But, more to the point perhaps, Ascension speaks to the one event in the life of Our Lord which is increasingly seen as part and parcel of the Resurrection and therefore as having already been celebrated on Easter morning. More and more we unconsciously seem to assume Resurrection and Ascension as the same and their occurrence as simultaneous.

If there is any part of the church's year which I would

like to have reasserted or any part of inevitable change that I would like to have arrested, it's the Ascension and the gradual absorption of it into the Resurrection, probably because at one stage of my growing up it meant everything to me.

14

So Much for Walt Disney

Spring and wealthy Chinamen were the only parts of my childhood that ever wrapped themselves up in brilliant colors in order to fold themselves away in death—the one in the militant greens and the other in the startling reds I loved so earnestly. And since there were far more springs than Chinamen dying in East Tennessee in the years between the world wars, I grew up assuming that, while both were acceptable, green at least was more normal in one's demise than red; and second, that somehow spring and China had a common origin and must, therefore, move toward a common destiny. Wherever that eventual destination was realized, I assumed it to be a place of carnival, full of firecrackers and colored torches illuminating an eternal night of benign cool and dogwood blooms, of smoke and dancing and lusty animals—a place where everyone wore red or green or both and looked through slightly slanted eyes out of plump young bodies. All of this was, of course, before I met Walt Disney or was old enough to see *Fantasia* and to begin to get the hang of things, so to speak.

I can remember yet the vividness of my shock when, sitting in the old Majestic Theatre one Saturday afternoon, I watched those final scenes in which Disney's ethereal angel-children float over misty meadows through banks of white flowers toward a pale opening in a pale sky. There was not one Pekingese dog or one paper dragon on the whole colorless screen. While the adults around me wept audibly, I watched, in the half-light, the faces of my two cousins, both of whom seemed totally unconcerned with either the dying or the crying, being far more involved in dividing the last of our popcorn between them. *Maybe,* I thought—the sniffling increasing as the procession grew fainter and whiter in its ascension—*maybe this is how it is if you die old, after living has already bleached you white; but if you die young, then maybe it's the colors and the carnival.* (Chinamen all looked to me to be without age and spring was obviously always young.)

I decided to set my mind to considering this solution in greater depth, probably because my grandmother was dying that summer of cancer, and both her progress and her color resembled the Disney progression across the misty meadows more than they resembled the brilliance of jonquils and tulips changing back into foliage and bulbs. Sure enough, Grandmother died that fall, and we put her in a white casket, surrounded her with unnaturally white flowers, and buried her during a funeral to which everyone except me wore black. I wore red.

My churching, up to this point, had been arduous and deliberate. In direct proportion to that adult effort and like all children, I had offered the opposition of polite disinterest and intellectual disengagement. But with the funeral and *Fantasia* coming up on each other so close like that, even a strong will had difficulty ignoring the obvious.

I was crossing through the hallway which led from the narthex to the Sunday school rooms one bleak

Sunday morning in November after Grandmother's funeral when I chanced to look up at the stained-glass window which rose two stories high behind the stairwell and illuminated the whole passageway. For the first time I perceived that the figure in the window was Christ's—his feet, on the bottom floor, floated above the haloed heads of the Apostles, and his arms were raised in blessing over the landing, while his head moved steadily upward toward the second-story ceiling and the hole of faded, cream glass in the curved arch of the window. I knew I was in trouble. I raced around the stair to the base of the window, climbed up on the window seat and, with difficulty, read the words, "Ascension Day—Gift of Dr. and Mrs. ———, May, 1929," on the brass plaque. Walt Disney *was* right! I never made it to Sunday school that day. In fact, I don't even remember making it to services. So much for paper dragons and fiery-winged cardinals and bobbing lanterns. Heaven was strictly Cream of Wheat and Ovaltine.

Given that kind of fall and winter and allowing for the fact that I had grown too old to feel comfortable with Easter baskets and somewhat doubtful bunny rabbits, I faced the coming spring and Holy Week with less enthusiasm than any child in my whole circle of cousins and acquaintances. In fact, I probably endured the most miserable Lent that any child has ever passed through . . . far worse, certainly, than what penitence itself would ever create for me later in adulthood. For distress of soul and mind, nothing could ever again approach the rigors of my ninth year. I had somehow made it, unasked, into existence, and I really didn't mind that. Life—at least my life—was not bad and seemed, as I watched the adult world around me, to offer several chances of getting better. What had me by the hair of my spiritual head, on that Lent, was that I could not find any way out of existence which was acceptable, which did not with its awesome pallor suck the joy out of the young days I had in hand.

We made it through Easter. I dyed eggs because everyone else did (even my father helping with the last batch), and because I loved beyond all other things at Easter the way my mother pickled beets on Easter Monday and then added the shelled and abandoned Easter eggs to the juice. The sight of the purply red eggs and the tart, cold beets on my Easter Monday dinner plate was the apex of the holiday for me every year, and I was not to be robbed of that pleasure even in this ninth and most dreadful year.

Ascension Day came and I shuddered in the warm, sunset light that streamed through the stairwell Christ, but either no one saw me or no one cared. And there, all alone in that corridor, the sounds of the congregation gathering beyond me for Ascension services and the pale Christ with his pale heaven floating above me, I experienced the shattering and totally engaging rebellion which is the beginning of mature religion, the first sign of honest grace. In later life I was to come to regard the distress of those moments and of that Lent in general as the labor pains of the soul which always precede new instruction, new stages of union. But there in that hallway and then in that young body, I had no previous experience by which to gauge what was happening to me. I only knew that the stained-glass Christ and the Walt Disney heaven were the same and that they were a lie. I knew that such a heaven was not worth living for, not worth creating creation for even. That God's death, the only one we could see for ourselves anyway, was the spring's blazing passage from pastel to green. I ran frantically out of that hallway and into the churchyard, throwing myself down on the new grass, its green staining my clothes and its crushed blades filling my nose with the bitter odor of spilled sap. There was real death to be part of every spring, and I was rolling in it, humming and throwing tufts of grass into the air and being nine again for the first time in weeks.

Pentecost came, of course, and tongues of gorgeous red fire blazed at me from the church bulletin, from the wall posters in the Sunday school rooms, from the hangings behind the altar. Red leaves pulled from the undersides of rosebushes decorated the altar, and only the baptismal candidates wore white. In another week the trappings were all changed to comfortable, brilliant green and reassuringly stayed that way until the anniversary of Grandmother's death when I was freshly turned ten and when our pastor preached on the dying of the church year, the folding away of the green to make way for Advent.

Afterward, being ten, I walked, rather than ran, out to the hallway at the end of the narthex. The Christ in the window was still pale and he definitely hadn't turned into a Chinaman yet, but I could have sworn, in that late November light, that he winked at me from his place above the landing. Whether he did or not really doesn't matter, of course. What matters is that at ten I thought he did, and it was the beginning of a long and consuming relationship between the two of us.

Postscript

It would be wrong of me to leave this book or to come away from these pages without saying one last time that they are, when all is finally said and done, about Easter. And that Easter is the straight stuff. It is hard-core Christianity.

We can all enjoy Christmas because it enjoys a distance from us. We have managed, in this world of many faiths and careless tolerations, to agree on a Lupercalia or Saturnalia in which we celebrate and exercise that which is most intellectually acceptable to our common definition of what humankind at its best should be. In proclaiming universal love and possible peace to each other for a few hours of the midwinter we absolve ourselves of the burden of hopelessness and perhaps of incipient godlessness; for Christmas can be shared by Christian and semi-Christian and flagrant pagan alike, all of us agreeing in its moral stances and cultural postures. Thank God we have such a day once a year.

But Easter is not so tractable. It is not about morality and the common good. It cannot be shared by the Christian with a Moslem fellow or a Jewish neighbor or a quasi-Christian. Nor can one write about Easter with the philosophical insights and enlightened self-interest of the professional moralist. Easter strips all of that away, and one is left naked of his abilities and his cleverness—and his dignity. One is left, ultimately, with Easter.

There is the mystery of eating this God, of incorporating him into oneself, body into body, a mystery so dark as to lie beyond the memory of humankind and beyond the reach of human poetry.

> "Verily, verily, I say unto you, Except ye eat the flesh of the Son of man, and drink his blood, ye have no life in you. Whoso eateth my flesh, and drinketh my blood, hath eternal life; . . . He that eateth my flesh, and drinketh my blood, dwelleth in me, and I in him. As the living Father hath sent me, and I live by the Father: so he that eateth me, even he shall live by me" (John 6:53–54, 56–57).

There is the mystery of the many realities, the lifting, however briefly, of the veil. "I beheld Satan as lightning fall from heaven" (Luke 10:18). And in the Garden, as reckless Peter comes to his defense, "Thinkest thou that I cannot now pray to my Father, and he shall presently give me more than twelve legions of angels?" (Matt. 26:53).

There is the mystery of death but briefly seen, the veil lifted here and there, in their three years together. But now, in this week of their ending, it is torn forever, leaving eleven men, five mourning women, one Roman centurion, and all of history with more than it can scarce summon the courage to acknowledge, much less act upon. Had he not already told them many times: "Your father Abraham rejoiced to see my day: and he saw it, and was glad. . . . Verily, verily, I say unto you, Before Abraham was, I am" (John 8:56, 58)? "Now that the dead are raised, even Moses showed at the bush, when he calleth the Lord the God of Abraham, and the God of Isaac, and the God of Jacob. For he is not a God of the dead, but of the living: for all live unto him" (Luke 20:37–38). And in his death cry amidst the renting of the Temple veil and the quaking of the earth, "the graves were opened; and many bodies of the saints which slept arose, and came out of the graves after his resurrection, and went into the holy city, and appeared unto many" (Matt. 27:52–53). Followed less than three days later with "touch me not; for I am not yet ascended to my Father: but go to my brethren, and say unto them, I ascend unto my Father, and your Father; and to my God, and your God" (John 20:17).

There is the mystery that, death having been penetrated and passage having been given through communion, the God, the divine Self, chooses to move into us. "And I will pray the Father, and he shall give you another Comforter, that he may abide with you for ever; even the Spirit of truth . . . ye know him; for he dwelleth with you, and shall be in you" (John 14:16, 17).

Then there is the final mystery, the one greater for me even than death itself. There is the mystery that this is God . . . that this Jew roaming the streets cursing fig trees and raging at money changers, healing children and feeding hundreds, calming winds and stopping storms, casting out devils and speaking to evil spirits is God . . . that this is what we claim to worship. That opening my mouth to receive the elements, bowing my head to pray, lifting my children up for baptism I claim all of this as God, as that of which I am, as process and cause and purpose, as mystery and master. To the extent that what I am can translate itself into words my mind can render to my fellows, this is what I am by virtue of grace and those very elements. This is Christianity, and it brooks little argument.